My Land Sings

Stories from the Rio Grande

RUDOLFO ANAYA

illustrated by AMY CÓRDOVA

MORROW JUNIOR BOOKS
NEW YORK

Published by Morrow Junior Books
a division of William Morrow and Company, Inc.
1350 Avenue of the Americas, New York, NY 10019
www.williammorrow.com

Printed in the United States of America.

10 9 8 7 6 5 4 3 2 1

Library of Congress Cataloging-in-Publication Data
Anaya, Rudolfo A.
My land sings: stories from the Río Grande / by Rudolfo Anaya; illustrated by
Amy Córdova.
p. cm.
Summary: A collection of ten original and traditional stories set in New Mexico,
including "Lupe and la Llorona," "The Shepherd Who Knew the Language of
Animals," and "Coyote and Raven."
ISBN 0-688-15078-0
1. New Mexico Juvenile fiction.   2. Children's stories, American.
3. Tales—New Mexico.   [1. New Mexico Fiction.   2. Short stories.
3. Folklore—New Mexico.]   I. Córdova, Amy, ill.
II. Title.   PZ7.A5186My 1999   [Fic]—dc21   99-19040   CIP

I dedicate these stories to the cuentistas, those wonderful storytellers from the Río Grande valley who kept our culture alive through our rich oral tradition. For centuries, they nurtured our imagination by telling the stories of our Hispanic and Indian ancestors.

I also dedicate the stories to young people everywhere. Listen to the stories of your elders so you may be in tune with the magic and beliefs contained in the folklore of your culture.

There are many people to acknowledge when one writes a collection of stories such as *My Land Sings.* Those who encouraged me as I worked on this project realize the importance of literature in the lives of young people. Many thanks to Patricia, Susan, and Ruth. They saw the stories grow and develop, and they kept the faith. Many thanks to José Griego y Maestas, who in 1980 asked me to translate some New Mexican cuentos from Spanish to English. That bilingual edition, *Cuentos: Tales from the Hispanic Southwest,* was published by the Museum of New Mexico Press in Santa Fe. As I explain in the Preface, five of the stories I retell here come from that collection.

Contents

℮
Preface

Dear Reader,

As a boy, I loved to hear people tell stories. In the evening, after the supper dishes were done, we would sit around the kitchen table and listen to the elders. Storytelling time was always magical. I had a favorite uncle who really knew how to spin a yarn, and when he came to visit, the evening became a storytelling feast.

To become enraptured in a story means you truly believe what happens in it. You feel as if you've "fallen into" the narrative. That's what I felt as a child, and this still happens to me today when I read or hear a good story.

Let me give you an example. It's a tale my father told a long time ago. When he was young, he was a vaquero, herding cattle on the llano, the eastern plain of New Mexico. One dark night, he and a friend were riding home on horseback when a ball of fire came bounding onto their path. Of course we knew that in the folklore of the Hispanic people of New Mexico witches were said to take the form of these bolas de lumbre. My father said he fired his pistol at the glowing apparition and it leapt away, disappearing into the darkness, leaving behind two very frightened cowboys.

I shivered as I listened, picturing the darkness on the plain, the rearing horses, and feeling my father's fear as he reached for his pistol and fired. They had come in contact with the unknown, and from that adventure his story evolved. My father's tone was serious, so I knew the story was true, and if it was true, then I, too, might one dark night run into a ball of fire when I played late along the river. I huddled closer to my sisters.

Outside, the brilliant New Mexican sunset colored the western clouds in red and gold; then dusk fell. Bats and nighthawks flitted in the dark, and an owl called by the river. Inside, our house, nestled near the Pecos River, was a safe haven. My hometown of Santa Rosa lay across the river; on this bank there were only our house and a couple of neighbors. In that world of stories told around the kitchen table, my imagination was nurtured.

I spent most summer evenings outside, playing with my friends. When it got late, someone might hear a strange noise and, half-joking, cry out, "La Llorona!" Many stories were told about this ghostly woman who appears at night along the river. Long ago, in a fit of rage and jealousy, she had murdered her children. Now she searches for them eternally, crying as she wanders the dark river paths. As children, we believed she was real. Feeling her presence made our hair stand on end, and we bolted and raced for home.

My imagination was nurtured in other ways. I loved the Saturday afternoon movies, and I read my share of comic books as a boy. But listening to a storyteller or reading a good book allows your mind to create images to fit the story; on the movie or television screen, they are provided for you. Your interaction with a story is personal, bringing into play your own imagination.

The stories I listened to as a child instilled in me a sense of belonging to a community and a knowledge of its values. Any event could become a story as the teller enhanced it with drama, and the beliefs of our people were woven into each tale. We may scoff at some beliefs and call them superstitions, but we must respect the body of knowledge each culture incorporates into its folk wisdom.

One evening, my uncle Pedro told of a man from Pastura who fell from his horse while rounding up cattle. As Uncle Pedro described the event, he embellished it, mentioning that the horse had been frightened by a whirlwind. Suddenly, the story came alive, for we all knew the devil rode the whirlwinds of the llano. The cowboy who was thrown from his horse, added my uncle Pedro, hadn't made the sign of the cross to ward off the evil in the whirlwind.

You don't have to believe this particular story, but you do have to understand that each community has its own folklore. You can believe parts or all, but either way folktales have a lot to teach about the world. And stories are continually being added to the pot. The tale my uncle told about the whirlwind began to spread, and each person who passed it on added new details. By the time it got back to the man who actually fell from the horse, he barely recognized himself. If that man's story is still being told today, I bet it's changed and grown even more elaborate.

In New Mexico, we have a rich Spanish and Native American folktale tradition. Spanish and Mexican settlers came to live near the Pueblo Indians of the Río Grande in 1598. From that meeting, a remarkable blending of culture and stories was born.

In Spanish, we call these stories cuentos. Among them are groups of stories about animals, riddles, humorous tales, and those that teach a lesson. The largest categories are tales of the pícaro and tales of enchantment. The pícaro in Spanish literature is a rogue or rascal. Enchantment stories have to do with magic or incantations. Some of these categories are combined in many stories. The people had an active imagination that was kept alive by storytelling.

At first, the cuentos were not written down. People memorized this vast storehouse of folktales and passed them down in the oral tradition, telling and retelling them. Since 1598, literally hundreds of cuentos have been preserved. By now, most have been collected by scholars and published. Since I grew up with both traditional cuentos and day-to-day storytelling, I thought this collection should include examples of both. Here you will find five cuentos I have retold and five of my own original stories.

In our folktales, there is a character who personifies death; her name is Doña Sebastiana. This old hag, who rides in a creaking cart, holding a bow and arrow, appears in New Mexican art and many folktales. The Spanish word for death is *la muerte,* and so when death is personified in our tales, she appears as Doña Sebastiana. Children who listen to stories about Doña Sebastiana learn about death's role in life.

Throughout our history, the rich imagination of New Mexicans has been constantly at work creating new cuentos and passing down the old ones. Sometimes they start with a simple question. Sometime, somewhere, a man or a woman asked: What if we could understand the language of animals? "The Shepherd Who Knew the Language of Animals" describes what happens to a person who receives this gift. But this cuento also asks another question: Is it right to keep a secret from the person you love the most?

The Spaniards and Mexicans who came to settle New Mexico were Roman Catholics, so many elements of that religion appear in the cuentos. Folktales around the world incorporate the spiritual values of the culture they come from. Just as the Greek gods are active characters in Greek myths, so the saints of the Catholic religion appear in the cuentos. In "The Three Brothers," it is the Virgin Mary and Jesus who appear to test the brothers.

Mary appears again in "The Lost Camel" to help a young man. In creating this version of "The Lost Camel," I took two cuentos and combined them. As a writer, I love to take traditional materials and combine them into new stories. This is something you can try. Take a myth or a legend you like and write it in your own words. It's like casting one of Shakespeare's plays in a contemporary setting. In fact, I recently saw a movie of *Romeo and Juliet* that did exactly this. We can enjoy both the traditional and the contemporary versions in different ways.

The setting of these stories is very important to me. I was born and raised in New Mexico, so I use its people, rivers, towns, mountains, and deserts in my writing. I set "The Lost Camel" and "The Miller's Good Luck" along the Río Grande. A great deal of the early history of New Mexico and the Southwest took place along this river. Mark Twain did the same with the Mississippi River, using it as a setting in his writing. In "Sipa's Choice," the river is so important the characters finally live *in* it.

The device of someone finding a diamond in the stomach of a fish probably stretches back to the origins of folktales in the Indian subcontinent. Thousands of years later, the idea appears with a New Mexican setting in "The Miller's Good Luck," in a story that instructs the young about saving for a rainy day. It's also meant to leave you

thinking: Does good luck or good planning rule our lives?

When I write my original stories, I try to capture the voice and drama of a good storyteller on the page. I often use characters from the oral tradition, like la Llorona. Versions of the crying woman appear in hundreds of stories in New Mexico, Mexico, and throughout Latin America. I think it's safe to say that this tragic woman is the best-known character in the Latino oral tradition.

Why am I so influenced by her? Would you believe me if I told you she chased me? One evening I had stayed too late in town, playing basketball with my friends, even though my mother had told me to be home before dark. While crossing the river, I heard la Llorona's cry, a horrible mournful shriek. I saw her bright eyes in the dark, felt her fingers clawing at me. I ran! I ran as I had never run before! Now when I tell this story, some people believe me, some don't, and others aren't sure. The point is that the characters of our cuentos feel *very* real to us. For me they are still alive.

Did you ever hear a story and couldn't get it out of your mind? For me, "Dulcinea" is such a story. Respect for the elders is an important value in our community, so we have many tales about children who don't obey their parents, including "Dulcinea." My father told me the bare outline of this young woman's story when I was twelve. Many years later, I included the story in my novel *Heart of Aztlán*. Then I wrote the version in this book. Now I think it would make an interesting movie. So you see, stories and characters take many forms. That's the beauty of storytelling.

By the way, there's also a very famous Mexican ballad about a disobedient son. "El Hijo Desobediente" tells the story of a young vaquero who disobeys his father, and for his transgression he dies at sunset. These ballads—songs that tell a story—are called corridos. Many stories are passed on in the form of corridos. It's my favorite form of Mexican music.

You might think "Coyote and Raven" is an original Native American tale. Well, Coyote and Raven are Native American characters, but this story about these characters is my own. Again, I first included a version of this story within a novel. I realized the story could stand on its own, so I retold it—with changes—in its present form for this book. I think you get the idea that I like to let my stories evolve.

"Coyote and Raven" is a story of how the world began. All Native Americans have fabulous tales of how they came from a prior world to this one. This story also explains why our dreams are so jumbled. You can try writing this form of traditional tale yourself to explain something in nature. Why do ducks quack? What are falling stars? Are ghosts real? How did rabbits get their long ears?

Stories can originate anywhere. That's certainly true for "The Fountain of Youth." In 1513, Ponce de León, the Spanish explorer, searched for the Fountain of Youth in Florida. Stories of the fountain circulated in Europe in the twelfth century; I took this story's theme and used it in the setting I know best. In my story, a young Spaniard obsessed with finding the fountain arrives in Mexico, then travels north to the Río Grande country. The question the story poses is whether we should search for eternal life. Should we live forever? And what are the consequences? Even stories set in past times have relevance today.

In my novel *Bless Me, Ultima,* I wrote an original legend to explain the huge golden carp that some kids see in the river. Students who read that novel always ask me about the legend. Did I make it up? What does it mean? Did I really see the golden carp?

I took some of the elements of the original story of the golden carp and created "Sipa's Choice," in which Sipa, a young man, ignores the traditional ways of his father. We face the same question today: As society changes, what do we keep of past values? Of course we won't be changed into golden fish if we make the wrong choices, but there are other consequences. What are they?

In many legends and myths from our culture and from around the world, the main character is often a man or a boy. Perhaps this is because the storytellers are often men. Maybe I wasn't around when my mother told stories with her sisters and friends. When I wrote "Lupe and la Llorona," I tried to think and act like Lupe. When you write your own stories, I urge you to put yourself in the shoes of your characters. Dare to create characters who aren't like you. The more we learn to think like other people, the better we understand them.

Stories help us understand and appreciate other people, and they hold many valuable lessons. It's exciting to be transported into the world created by a story. Reading is one of the best ways to stimulate your creativity. I hope you remain a reader all your life.

Your friend,
Rudolfo Anaya

My Land Sings

Stories from the Rio Grande

Lupe and la Llorona

When the clock in the kitchen struck midnight, Lupe quietly got out of bed. She dressed hurriedly, crept to her bedroom door, and listened intently. In the adjacent bedroom, her parents were sound asleep.

Quietly, she slipped out of the house. The village of Puerto de Luna, a farming community on the banks of the Pecos River, was also asleep. An October quarter-moon hung over the valley, but it shed very little light. Lupe shivered as she ran to meet Carlos by the church.

Earlier that afternoon in the schoolyard, Carlos had been bragging that he wasn't afraid of la Llorona.

"It's just a story our parents tell to scare us," he said to the seventh graders gathered around him.

"No, she's real," one of the girls replied.

"I don't believe it," Carlos said, looking at Lupe. "I dare anyone to go to the river with me."

"At midnight?"

"Yes, at midnight!"

The others glanced nervously at Lupe. She was strong and tall like Carlos, and she was the only one in the group who stood up to him.

"It's a crazy idea," Lupe said.

"What's the matter, you chicken?"

Lupe clenched her teeth. Carlos had been after her all week, ever since her team had beaten his in baseball. She had tried not to pay attention to his needling, but nobody called her chicken!

"I'll prove who's chicken," she shot back. "I'll go with you tonight!"

The kids had cheered her, but later, as they walked back to the classroom, José fell in step beside Lupe. He was her neighbor, and the boy she secretly admired.

"You don't have to go," he whispered. "It's dangerous by the river at night."

"Do you mean it's too dangerous for a girl?"

José blushed. "You know what I mean."

"I know," Lupe answered. "But Carlos dared me in front of the gang. I won't let Carlos call me a coward."

"Yeah," José agreed. He knew Carlos had been hassling Lupe all week. "Do you want me to go with you?" he offered.

"No, Carlos challenged me." She looked into his eyes and saw he really was concerned about her. "Thanks," she added.

José shrugged. "Just be careful" were his parting words.

Maybe I'm like Carlos, Lupe thought as she approached the church at midnight. I want to find out if la Llorona is real or just a story our parents tell. She stopped cold when she spotted a shadow at the door. Her skin tingled. "Who is it?" she called.

"Booooo!" Carlos cried, jumping out at her.

"Boo yourself!" Lupe said, faking laughter to show he hadn't frightened her.

"Bet you thought it was la Llorona," Carlos teased her.

"Don't be silly," Lupe answered boldly.

"Are you afraid?" asked Carlos, peering toward the river.

Lupe hesitated. All her life, she had heard the different stories people told about la Llorona. Some said she was a young woman who long ago had lived in a neighboring village. She had fallen in love with a rich man's son and had a baby, but since she wasn't married to him, the young man's parents were going to take the baby away from her. The baby was all the poor girl had in the world, and she vowed not to let them take it.

When the family came with the sheriff for the child, the young woman gathered the baby in her arms and fled to the river. The sheriff and his deputies followed, using hound dogs to track her. The baying of the dogs could be heard up and down the valley.

As the sheriff and his men drew near, the frightened girl threw herself into the river. The strong current swept her off her feet and tore the baby from her arms. It disappeared into the watery depths.

Later, some villagers would say she had intentionally thrown the baby into the river. The sheriff had saved the young woman, but the baby drowned. It was never found.

After the accident, the young woman was overcome with grief. She walked along the edge of the river, looking for her baby. At night, the people of the village heard her crying and calling the child's name.

"You can still hear her crying at night," the old people told the children. "She became la Llorona, 'the crying woman.' Don't go near the water. She might think you are her child and take you."

Parents told the story to warn their children not to play near the river and its dangerous currents.

"I'm not afraid," Lupe said, shivering. She wasn't going to let Carlos scare her. Besides, she had the medal of her guardian angel hanging around her neck. She touched it and said a silent prayer.

Carlos, too, had hesitated. Across the road, the river and its dark forest looked menacing. "Okay, let's go," he said.

They left the village and hurried through the river bosque. Overhead, the tall, stately cottonwood trees formed a canopy that shut out the scant moonlight. Around them, river willows and salt cedars pressed in on the thin trail. Finally, they came to a small clearing in the brush.

"Here's where she cries at night," Carlos said.

Lupe shivered. She knew the spot. This was the place where the young woman and her baby had jumped into the river.

There was something evil about the place. Dank vapors rose from the river. The awful stink of something dead touched Lupe's nostrils. The trees rose in the dark like giant specters.

Suddenly, they heard an eerie sound and they froze. A shadow appeared in the moonlight and shimmered on the water. It seemed to be the figure of a young woman walking on the water, coming toward them. A shrill noise filled the night, sounding like the cry of a grieving woman.

Shivers ran down Lupe's spine as the shadow seemed to reach out to grab them. "Oh, my God!" she cried.

"La Llorona!" Carlos shouted, and he turned and ran. Lupe followed. With adrenaline pumping in their bodies, they ran as they never had before. Branches whipped at them as they stumbled through the brush. Behind them, they heard the icy cry of la Llorona. Lupe and Carlos didn't stop until they were safely back at the church.

From the door, they looked back toward the river.

"It was la Llorona!" Carlos gasped, panting for breath. "But she can't come here!"

Lupe, too, was out of breath, and she was shivering, but she wasn't sure if it was la Llorona she had seen or a shadow. And the cry could have been the screech of an owl or cats roaming the river's edge. Sometimes cats' cries sounded almost human.

"You ran!" Lupe exclaimed.

"You did, too!" Carlos shot back, his voice trembling.

"You were scared."

Carlos nodded. "Don't tell the others."

"I won't," Lupe promised, but she was disappointed they had run. They should have stayed to see if the shadow really was la Llorona.

"I gotta go," Carlos said, and he bolted down the street toward home.

Lupe, still shivering, also ran home. She quietly let herself in the house and crawled into bed, but she couldn't sleep. All night, she kept seeing the shadow of the weeping river woman. She did have one satisfaction: Carlos had run, too.

"He isn't any braver than me," Lupe said to herself; then she fell asleep, saying a prayer of thanks to her guardian angel.

In the morning, she was too sleepy to get up at the usual time. Her mother finally had to pull her out of bed. She was late for school.

During recess, the kids were eager to learn if Lupe and Carlos had gone to the river.

"I saw her," Carlos bragged. "I wasn't afraid of her."

"Did you see her?" José asked Lupe.

Lupe didn't know how to reply. Carlos had lied. She wanted to tell everyone they had run, but she couldn't.

"Yeah, I saw her," Lupe mumbled, and walked away. She knew Carlos would soon be telling the gang that only he, Carlos, had been the brave one. But Lupe didn't care.

When she returned home in the afternoon, she hurried to help her father with the chores.

"Why are you so lazy today?" her father asked as he milked the cow and Lupe gathered the eggs in the chicken coop.

"I didn't sleep well, I guess," she replied, knowing she had lied again. "Father," she asked, "is there really a Llorona?"

"Oh yes," her father answered. "She lives by the river, and if you misbehave, she'll get you." He winked.

"I try to be good," Lupe said.

"I know. But I think your mom is right; you have to start acting like a girl."

"Why?"

"Well, you can't be a tomboy forever. You're changing."

Lupe knew she was changing. Playing games with the boys on the playground wasn't as much fun anymore. Even proving to Carlos she could keep up with him had lost its sense of adventure. But la Llorona intrigued her.

"Why does she cry?" Lupe asked. She knew the story, but each time she heard it, there seemed to be a new twist.

"Some people say la Llorona was a young woman who drowned her baby. When the woman died, St. Peter told her she couldn't enter heaven until she brought the soul of her baby with her. So her spirit came back to earth. She cries as she searches the river, looking for the child she can never find."

Lupe was intrigued by her father's version of the story. She always loved to hear his stories. He knew all the old cuentos.

"But is she real?" Lupe asked.

"Who knows?" her father answered. "Some people claim they've seen her."

"Have you?"

Her father shook his head. "No."

He lifted the bucket of milk and Lupe picked up the basket of eggs she had gathered. Together, they walked toward the house, where Lupe's mother had a hot supper ready.

"I guess if you want to find out the truth about la Llorona, you're going to have to meet her yourself," her father said.

Was he teasing? Lupe wondered.

"And don't forget, this Saturday is the fiesta," he added.

"How can I?" Lupe replied. "Mother's sewing me a new dress. I'm supposed to act like a lady and dance."

Her father laughed. "Save a dance for me."

"I will."

Every year, the village celebrated the feast of its patron saint. There were games and dancing. People came from other villages to participate in the fiesta. This year was different. Lupe would dress like a young woman and dance with the boys who asked her.

"Are los Abuelos coming this year?" she asked.

"Seguro que sí," her father replied. "Los Abuelos come to make sure the kids have been behaving. If you're naughty, they might grab you."

"Are you going to be one of the Abuelos?"

"Can't tell you. Just remember to be good. Some children think they're too grown-up to listen to their parents. Those are the ones the Abuelos are after."

Lupe wondered if her father knew she had slipped out of the house last night.

She remembered how frightened she had been when she first saw the Abuelos. She was six and her parents had taken her to church. After Mass, the Abuelos came walking down the street, cracking their whips. Lupe was so scared, she ran to hide behind her mother's skirt.

Now she wasn't afraid of los Abuelos. She knew they were men from the village who wore masks on their faces. They cracked their whips to scare the children into good behavior. But la Llorona? Lupe still wasn't sure if she was real or just a story. She had to prove to herself that she wasn't afraid of la Llorona. She would go alone to the river, tonight.

That night, Lupe slipped out of bed again and dressed without a sound. Then she headed for the river and entered the bosque. The shadows were thicker than she remembered. Occasional bird cries sounded in the darkness, and tree branches moved in the breeze.

She was in a very dark area of the path when she heard something behind her. Someone was following her. She walked faster and tried to whistle a tune, but the sound wouldn't come out. She wished she hadn't left the safety of her bed. Maybe Carlos was right; maybe last night they *had* seen la Llorona.

Lupe turned a corner in the trail and there in front of her stood the figure of a woman. She was dressed in a long, tattered dress. Her tangled hair fell over her shoulders, nearly to the ground. Her eyes were red from crying. She raised her arms and Lupe saw her sharp fingernails. Then her terrible cry filled the night, and Lupe's blood turned to ice. Her knees quivered.

She turned to run, but she hit her head on the branch of a tree and fell to the ground. Just before she passed out, she felt the arms of la Llorona lifting her up.

When Lupe opened her eyes, she found herself in a dark cavern. A small fire illuminated two figures who sat in front of the flickering light. They turned to look at her, and Lupe saw two of the scariest monsters she had ever imagined.

Lupe trembled with fright. "La Llorona," she gasped.

"Yes, I am the creature they call la Llorona," the woman in the tattered dress answered.

"And who is he?" Lupe asked, pointing at the monster with the huge head and red eyes. His nose was long and green. At the ends of his large arms dangled two big hands. In one hand he held a whip, in the other a sack. His gnarled legs were like old tree trunks in the dim light.

"This is the Coco Man," la Llorona said. "Some call him el Kookoóee."

Lupe had heard some of the old people tell stories about this bogeyman. Now she knew the Coco Man was real. She shivered, wondering if they planned to eat her alive.

"I want to go home," she whispered.

"You will," replied la Llorona, "in due time. We brought you here for a reason."

"Why?" Lupe asked.

"We want you to know our story and tell it to your friends."

"My friends are afraid of you," Lupe said, drawing close to the warmth of the fire. The two creatures of the night weren't so scary after all.

"Are you afraid of us?" la Llorona asked.

"No," Lupe replied.

"Only naughty children should be afraid of us," said la

Llorona. "It is true that I cry by the river at night, but only because I am looking for my child."

"And him?" Lupe asked, meaning the giant Coco Man, who still sat quietly by the fire.

"El Coco is a creature of the river forest."

"Why does he have a sack?"

"He throws misbehaving children in the sack. But if you're good, you don't have to worry. Actually, he's a very good son."

"Is he the baby who drowned?" Lupe blurted.

"No. El Coco is an adopted son. One day, I was walking near here and I met Don Cuervo, the crow. Don Cuervo felt sorry I could not find my drowned child, so he told me about a secret cave in which I would find a creature of the forest. I went to the cave and inside I found a bundle. I unwrapped it, and there was el Coco. He was an orphan, so I became the mother of the Kookoóee."

"You raised el Coco?" Lupe asked.

"Yes."

"What does he do?"

"He makes sure naughty children obey their parents."

The giant figure of the Kookoóee stood up, his head almost touching the roof of the cave. His jaws opened, showing teeth like those of a great white shark, and his eyes flashed fire. His long arms reached out like tree branches.

Lupe jumped back in terror.

"Tell the children to be good," the Kookoóee said, and

he cracked his whip. The sound echoed like thunder in the cave.

"I will!" Lupe cried. "I will!" She struggled to get up and run, but her arms seemed pinned to the ground.

"Don't move!" a voice said. "It's okay."

"El Coco!" Lupe shouted, thrashing out and trying to run.

"Lupe!" somebody called to her. "It's me. Stop fighting!" It was her father, kneeling and holding her in his arms.

Lupe opened her eyes. Her mother knelt by her. Behind them stood people from the village.

"My child," her mother comforted her. "You hit your head, but you're all right now. Gracias a Dios."

"We've been looking all morning for you," said her father.

"What happened?" Lupe asked.

"You must have hit your head on a tree branch," her father explained.

"What were you doing at the river? Alone?" her mother asked.

"I saw la Llorona and the Kookoóee! They were in a cave!"

Her father laughed. "You had a dream. A nightmare."

"No!" Lupe insisted. "I saw them! They're real."

Her mother felt the bump on Lupe's head. "Try to be still, mi hija. We need to get you home where you can rest. You'll realize it was just a bad dream."

Was it a nightmare? Lupe wondered. It seemed so real. Should she tell her friends? She had thought la Llorona and the Kookoóee were only creatures from the old stories.

Perhaps Carlos and the other boys who cut school and went to the river to smoke had seen la Llorona because they were misbehaving. If you obeyed your parents, you didn't see these creatures.

Lupe had sneaked out at night. Maybe that's why la Llorona and el Coco had appeared to her.

"You're fine," her father said, and lifted her in his arms. "A little rest and you'll be ready for the fiesta."

Lupe rested all day. When she slept, she saw the Kookoóee in her dreams, but they weren't threatening dreams. The Coco Man cracked his whip, creating a wind that swept over the cottonwood trees along the river. Then he dissolved into the green forest, becoming like a tree.

The next day at school, all the kids surrounded Lupe. They knew she had been lost and that the entire village had searched for her.

"Why did you go to the river?" asked José.

Lupe couldn't bring herself to say that she had wanted to prove she wasn't afraid. But her true motive was that she had wanted to know if la Llorona was real or not.

"What did you see?" asked Carlos.

"I saw la Llorona and the Coco Man," Lupe replied. She hoped José wouldn't laugh at her.

"You saw the Kookoóee!"

"No way!" Carlos shook his head.

"Did you really see him?" one of the kids asked.

"Yes." Lupe nodded.

"I believe you," José said.

"Ah, there's no such thing as the Kookoóee," Carlos scoffed. "You're making it up."

"I saw him," Lupe insisted. "He lives in a cave with la Llorona! He has a long nose, big teeth, and legs that look like tree trunks! He cracks a whip just like the Abuelos!"

The other kids nodded. Maybe Lupe was telling the truth.

"If you saw him, show him to us," Carlos said. "Let's go to the river right now."

"Yeah," one of his friends said, "let's play hooky."

"How about it, Lupe?" Carlos asked.

Lupe shook her head. She didn't want to cut school.

"She doesn't have to prove anything," said José.

"She's chicken," Carlos said.

"I'm not chicken!" Lupe shouted, and pushed Carlos. He pushed back, and they fell to the ground, rolling around and punching at each other until a teacher separated them. The teacher grabbed them and took them to the principal. Both had to stay after school and clean the chalkboards.

The next day was miserable for Lupe. The kids teased her. "Where's the Kookoóee?" they joked. Only José remained loyal. He believed Lupe.

* * *

On Saturday, the whole village attended the fiesta. People dressed in their best clothes. After Mass at the church, there was a feast. Everyone brought food, and musicians came to play for the dance. The children played tag and kick the can. All day, the fiesta continued; then late in the afternoon, as the sun was about to set, someone shouted that the Abuelos were coming.

Carlos hid behind the church. He had filled balloons with water to throw at the Abuelos.

Down the street came three old men dressed in jeans and boots like scruffy cowboys, wearing masks and cracking their whips.

"Los Abuelos!" the smaller children cried, and ran to hide behind their mothers. The loud popping of the whips and the strange sight of the Abuelos frightened them.

Carlos shouted, "I'm not afraid of the Abuelos!" and threw a water balloon.

The water splashed on one of the Abuelos' boots. The startled Abuelo cracked his whip, but Carlos only laughed.

"¡Ay, muchacho malo!" the mud-splattered Abuelo cried. He chased Carlos, but the boy zigzagged through the crowd and hid.

The Abuelos shook their heads and continued down the road.

"You shouldn't have done that," José said.

"Ah, they're just three old men dressed up with masks," Carlos replied.

"The Kookoóee might get you."

"He ain't real," Carlos answered.

"He is," Lupe said. She was sure her father was one of the men playing the part of an Abuelo, the one Carlos had hit with the balloon.

"Prove it!"

"Follow me to the cave by the river," Lupe said, daring Carlos and the kids who stood behind him.

"Nah, it's getting dark," one of the boys said. "My parents don't let me go to the river when it's dark."

"Let's settle this once and for all," Carlos said. "I'll go."

"This time, I'll go, too," José said.

Lupe nodded. "All right. Just the three of us."

"We'll wait here," one of the boys said. "If you chicken out and run, we'll know."

"Vamos," Lupe said, and led Carlos and José to the river. They entered the dark trail under the giant cottonwoods.

They were quickly swallowed by the gloomy darkness and failed to realize they were being followed. Lupe sensed something and looked back, but the path was empty. Only briefly did she think she had seen the figures of the Abuelos.

"What is it?" asked José, standing close to her and looking tentatively into the dark.

"Nothing."

"Maybe we should turn back," Carlos suggested.

"Don't be chicken," Lupe teased him.

She led them forward until they came to the cave.

"We're here," Lupe said. "Look." She pointed to the cave in the cliff. "That's where I saw la Llorona and the Kookoóee!"

"I don't see anything," Carlos said. "We can go home now."

Suddenly, a loud cry and the crack of a whip made them jump.

"What was that?" Carlos cried, grabbing Lupe's arm.

The figure of a woman appeared in front of them, her tattered white dress floating back and forth.

"La Llorona!" Carlos screamed.

Behind the eerie shape of the woman, the tree branches shook, and a giant figure came crashing through the thick brush. Looming above them in the dark, he was tall as a tree, and his eyes burned brightly. His big jaw opened, exposing sharp teeth. In one huge hand, he held a bag; with his other hand, he cracked his whip.

"El Coco!" Carlos gasped. He turned and ran.

The long, piercing cry of la Llorona filled the night, but Lupe held her ground. She smiled as she looked up at the huge figure swinging from side to side.

Then she heard someone laugh, a laughter that sounded very much like her father's. In the dark, she caught a glimpse of one of the Abuelos holding up the dummy they had dressed as el Coco. Another held a white dress raised on a pole, the fluttering dress Carlos had mistaken for la Llorona.

With one final frightful scream, the figures of the

Kookoóee and la Llorona drew back into the darkness and disappeared.

"Los Abuelos," José said. He had stood by Lupe while Carlos ran.

"Yes." Lupe smiled. "I think they came to teach Carlos a lesson."

"Were you afraid?" asked José.

"A little," Lupe confessed.

"But you didn't run. Carlos ran."

"Carlos pretends he's braver than he is," Lupe replied. "Come on. Let's get back to the fiesta. My mother wants me to go to the dance tonight."

"And I'm hungry," José said.

As they started back toward the village, Lupe turned to her friend. "By the way, José, I'll save a dance for you tonight."

Dulcinea

Dulcinea lived with her parents on the Llano Estacado, a wide and grassy plain. Their home was a comfortable but humble house constructed of adobe, mud bricks made from the earth. The pitched roof was tin, and when it rained, the pelting sound on the tin became a lulling crescendo.

The homes on the llano were far apart, so few neighbors came to visit Dulcinea's family. Once in a while, a shepherd drove his flock near their home on the way to new pastures. Then the man would stop to talk with Dulcinea's father, exchanging information on the grass, weather, the price of sheep, and supplies.

Otherwise, the families of the llano met only at

church. On Sundays when he was home, Dulcinea's father would hitch his horse to the buggy and he, his wife, and his daughter would go to church in the village of Las Pasturas.

Like most of the men on the llano, Dulcinea's father owned a flock of sheep, which he grazed in the grasslands. Often he was gone for days, shepherding his herd across the llano in search of good grass and water.

Dulcinea spent her days with her mother, a quiet woman who was accustomed to the loneliness of the llano. She taught Dulcinea how to care for their home.

The father kept a cow in a corral near the house, and Dulcinea had to get up every morning to milk her. She also collected the eggs laid by the chickens.

Dulcinea's strict parents didn't allow her to attend school, but her mother had taught her to read the Bible. Sometimes, as they sat embroidering, her mother would break her silence and explain one of the Bible stories. Dulcinea also secretly read the Sears catalog her father picked up once a year in the village. She flipped through the pages, looking at the women's clothing, and she dreamed of traveling to distant lands.

Life on the wide expanse of llano was lonely. Sometimes in the afternoon when their housework was done and her mother was napping, Dulcinea walked on the llano. She went as far as she dared, then turned to look back at the house. On the wide llano, the home appeared as a speck. Dulcinea would lie on the warm grass and daydream.

Overhead, vultures circled in the sky. Grasshoppers chirped in the afternoon heat. Sometimes she heard a coyote cry. If she listened very closely, she thought all the small sounds of the llano were gathered into one. She would close her eyes and let the warmth of the sun and the earth carry her into a dizzying, enjoyable dream.

Once in a long while, one of her girlfriends who lived in the village would come with her mother to visit. This was a favorite time for Dulcinea, because they would spend hours rummaging through a trunk Dulcinea's aunt had left her when she died. The girls would dress in the satin dresses they found in the trunk, hum tunes, and dance.

As she grew older, Dulcinea envied the social life of the village girls. They attended school, they could meet at the village store after school, and sometimes they got to drive to Santa Rosa or Vaughn with their parents.

Dulcinea looked forward to attending church, because there she could visit with other girls. She would catch up with her friends' adventures, the small, simple experiences that were part of every girl's life, things that seemed exciting compared to Dulcinea's quiet life on the llano.

One Sunday, Dulcinea and her family arrived at the church to find the villagers excited by the arrival of a young stranger. No one knew his business, but he appeared to be very rich.

When Dulcinea alighted from the buggy, she saw the stranger across the road from the church, seated on his spirited black horse. He was dressed in a black silk suit and black hat. His dark eyes held Dulcinea's for an instant, and Dulcinea felt a chill run through her body.

Dulcinea's friends ran to meet her.

"Isn't he handsome!" one girl exclaimed as she stole a glance at the stranger.

"They say he's looking for a wife," another girl said.

"Dulcinea is only fifteen, too young to think of marriage," her mother said, and drew her daughter away. But at the door of the simple adobe church, Dulcinea turned and caught one last glimpse of the stranger. He tipped his hat and smiled. His gaze told her he knew the secret desires in her heart.

She felt her heart skip a beat. Her mother and father moved ahead, and Dulcinea entered the church with her friends pressing around her.

"He looked at you!" one girl whispered. "You're blushing."

Dulcinea had felt a chill when the stranger's eyes caught hers, but her cheeks were warm.

"Are you coming to the dance this Saturday?" another asked as they found their pews.

"There's a rumor he'll attend," whispered a third.

At that instant, Dulcinea made a resolution. She wanted to meet the stranger whose gaze burned her heart. She was tired of the llano. She was fifteen, and that meant she was a woman. She must think about her future. Something in the stranger's eyes told her there was another life, one far more interesting than life on the llano.

"Yes," Dulcinea answered. "I'll be there."

Her response surprised her. She knew she needed her parents' permission to attend a dance, but her heart told her that one way or another, she was destined to meet the stranger who rode the black horse.

Dulcinea loved to dance. At the community fiestas, she met the young men of the village. They weren't very good dancers, but, attracted by her beauty, they flocked to her.

Dulcinea had always been accompanied to the village fiestas by her parents. They were old-fashioned, and every boy who wanted to dance with their daughter had to ask their permission first. Of course, when her father was away with the sheep, she and her mother didn't attend any of the gatherings.

That morning on the way home from church, Dulcinea mentioned the dance to her parents. "Please, can we go?" she asked.

"No," her father responded.

"Why not?" Dulcinea asked.

"The men say there are bad omens in the air. They say a dark wind follows the stranger who has come to our village. My father used to say that the devil rides the whirlwind."

"It's true," Dulcinea's mother said, gazing back at the dark whirlwind that seemed to be following them. She made the sign of the cross in its direction and it swerved away, disappearing in the distance.

"Besides," her father continued, "I'll be gone with the sheep this week, so you must stay home with your mother."

Dulcinea said no more. She had never disobeyed her parents, nor even argued with her father, but all that week she thought of the dance.

One night in the privacy of her room, she looked in the mirror as she readied herself for bed. She had never thought of herself as beautiful, but now the dark eyes looking out from her oval face told her she was attractive. She admired herself, and what she saw made her tingle. Then she saw the dark stranger's eyes in the mirror.

Dulcinea gasped and drew back.

"Don't be afraid," said the voice in the mirror. "I have come to take you with me. Come to the dance."

Dulcinea shivered, then drew close to the mirror. The stranger's eyes were gone, but she was sure she had heard him. She sniffed the air and thought she smelled sulfur.

"Yes," she said to herself as she got into bed. "I will go to the dance."

Early the next day, her father left with his flock. In the afternoon, a young shepherd by the name of Benito stopped by Dulcinea's home. He made the excuse of asking for a drink of water, but he had another purpose.

Dulcinea stepped outside and held the bucket of water while Benito ladled a drink. He was shy. He talked about the weather and his sheep.

Finally, he asked, "Are you going to the dance?"

"Yes," Dulcinea replied.

"Will you save the last dance for me?" he asked bravely.

The custom was that the last dance was danced by married couples, or couples who were serious about each other, those planning to marry.

"Perhaps," Dulcinea said, without committing herself.

Benito thanked her for the water. "Gracias. I'll wait for the last dance."

"Adiós," Dulcinea said. She watched as he led his flock into the vast plain.

If I stay here, Dulcinea thought, looking at the empty landscape, I will marry someone like Benito. And my future will be as lonely as my mother's. Life would be so different with the stranger whose smile melted my heart.

On Saturday mornings, Dulcinea's chore was to go to the spring for drinking water. She hitched her father's horse to the old cart. A large wooden barrel sat on the cart. Then she slowly made her way across the empty grassland to the spring at Agua Negra.

At the spring, Dulcinea worked hard, using a bucket to fill the barrel. When she was done, she knelt to drink and splash cool water on her forehead. The water revived her.

She gazed across the llano and saw a cloud of dust in the distance. Realizing she had been thinking about the dance while she worked, she danced around the spring, gliding faster and faster, until her long black hair tore loose from its ribbons and swirled in the wind. Exhausted, she fell to the ground.

"I will go to the dance!" she cried, gasping for breath.

At that moment, a whirlwind swept down on her, and Dulcinea cowered in fear.

The wind swept around her, crying mournfully. A flash of lightning tore across the sky, followed by thunder, but there were no clouds in sight. Dulcinea covered her eyes and shivered as the wind tore at her clothes. Nearby, her horse trembled and whinnied in fear.

Then the wind grew calm, and Dulcinea looked up and saw the stranger on his spirited black horse, standing in front of her. He sat like a king, a broad black hat shading his face. On his hands, he wore white gloves.

He smiled and called her name.

"How did you know my name?" she asked, clutching at the cart as she stood up.

"I know many secrets," the stranger said. "I know you love to dance."

"Yes, I do," Dulcinea answered, feeling an exciting tremor in her body.

"Then come to the dance tonight, and I will dance only with you."

"Yes, I will come," Dulcinea answered.

"I will wait for you," the stranger said, spurring his horse and disappearing into the whirlwind that swept westward.

Dulcinea felt shaken. She quieted her horse, which stood trembling in its harness.

The stranger has promised to dance only with me, she thought as she retied her hair. Yes, I will dance all night in his arms.

She hurried home to make plans.

"I was worried for you," her mother said, taking the bucket of fresh water from Dulcinea. "A dark wind full of fury passed over the house. I was afraid."

"There is nothing to fear," Dulcinea replied.

"What took you so long?"

"I stopped to play with the lambs," Dulcinea said, surprised to find herself lying to her mother for the first time in her life.

Her mother dipped a cup into the water and screamed. Resting at the bottom of the bucket was an ugly toad. It stuck out its tongue, which was forked like a snake's.

"¡Dios mío!" her mother screamed, and ran to the door. She threw the bucket as far as she could. She made the sign of the cross to ward off evil, and the toad disappeared.

"What have you done?" Dulcinea's mother asked, horrified.

Dulcinea lied again. "It must have crawled into the bucket while I was playing with the lambs."

"We must pray," her mother said, turning to the small altar she kept in the corner.

Dulcinea stopped her. "No. I don't have time. I'm going to the dance."

"Your father forbids it," her mother said.

"But he's not here. He's away with the sheep. And I am going!"

"I forbid you!" her mother exclaimed. "I won't let you go out tonight. Don't you see the evil signs around us?"

"I will go!" Dulcinea said in a harsh tone.

She rushed to her room and closed the door, then looked at herself in the mirror.

"I'm old enough to do as I please," she said to the mirror. "Why should my mother's fear keep me from the dance? This is my chance to meet someone who isn't a shepherd. I won't throw this opportunity away."

Dulcinea opened her aunt's trunk. It held the fine satin dresses her aunt had worn as a young woman. Dulcinea picked out a red dress with white fringe. She polished her boots and laced them tight. Then she sat before the mirror, and, for the first time, put on dark red lipstick, which she also had found in the trunk. She combed out her long black hair and let it fall loose over her shoulders.

When she stepped out of her room, her mother gasped.

"Oh, you look beautiful," she said. "You remind me of my sister, wearing her dress. How she loved to dance. But please don't go. I have a feeling something terrible will happen."

"Don't you understand? It's lonely here," Dulcinea answered. "Tonight I want to dance with the handsome stranger. I must go."

Dulcinea's mother knew life on the llano was lonely for her daughter, but tonight she was very fearful. She shook her head.

"Then I will go without your permission," Dulcinea said. She walked out to the corral, hitched her father's horse to the buggy, and rode away.

It was dusk as she started for the village. A chilling wind swept across the llano, and dark storm clouds gathered in the west. Bats flitted around her, and in the distance the coyotes cried.

Darkness fell as Dulcinea urged her father's horse onward. Overhead, the new moon provided little light.

When Dulcinea arrived at the village, she could hear the music coming from the dance hall. She hurried inside. Families crowded the room, and many couples were already dancing. In the corner, a fiddler, a guitarist, and a man with an accordion alternated waltzes with polkas.

Dulcinea saw the stranger standing in a dark corner of the dance hall. He smiled and stepped out of the shadows to bow before her.

"I have been waiting," he said, taking her hand.

Dulcinea curtsied, and everyone turned to watch. As before, the stranger was dressed impeccably in a black silk suit and white gloves. The people of the village had never seen anyone dressed so elegantly.

Dulcinea, too, looked charming. Neighbors who had known her since childhood marveled at her beauty. "No doubt," one woman whispered, "she looks like her aunt, not her mother."

"But where are her parents?" the woman's friend asked. Dulcinea had come alone.

She and the stranger made a handsome couple. They stepped out onto the middle of the floor and whirled about as if they were dancing on clouds.

As they waltzed around the room, he whispered, "I'm glad you didn't listen to your mother."

"How did you know?" Dulcinea asked.

"I know all your secrets," he replied.

"And I don't even know your name."

"I will tell you at midnight."

"And will you take off your gloves?"

"I will at midnight." He smiled. "But only if you promise to dance the midnight dance with me."

"I promise," Dulcinea answered, glancing toward a very sad Benito, who turned and left the room.

Dulcinea and the stranger danced till the clock struck midnight. Then Dulcinea held up her hand and stopped the dance.

"It's midnight," she announced, "and the stranger has promised to tell me his name and to take off his gloves. And I will dance the midnight dance with him."

She turned to the stranger, and he smiled.

"Yes, I keep my bargains," he said, and slowly took off his white gloves.

As he did so, the people fell back in horror. The hands of the stranger were shaped like the hooves of a goat. They were cloven and covered with coarse hair.

Dulcinea screamed and turned to run, but the stranger pulled her into his arms.

"You promised me this dance," he said, and held her tightly. "The Dance of the Devil!"

He swirled her around the dance floor, and Dulcinea, frozen with terror, could only follow.

The people and musicians also cried in horror when they saw the cloven hooves of the devil. Everyone rushed for the door. Only one man pushed past the frightened crowd— Dulcinea's father.

Hours earlier, he had arrived home with his flock, to be met by his wife with the tale of Dulcinea's disobedience. He had hurried to the dance hall, arriving in time to see the stranger remove his gloves.

He rushed forward to help his daughter, carrying his shepherd's staff, which had a cross carved on one end.

"In the name of God, release my daughter!" Dulcinea's father cried, and struck at the stranger.

When the cross touched the stranger, he screamed in pain and disappeared in a cloud of sulfurous smoke. Dulcinea fell crying to the floor.

Her father gathered her in his arms, carried her outside to the buggy, and took her home. He and his wife tried to comfort their daughter, but the girl could not rest.

All night, she tossed and turned.

"I disobeyed my parents," she moaned over and over.

"We forgive you," her mother replied, trying to assuage the fever that burned in her daughter.

"All is forgiven," her father agreed.

But Dulcinea still couldn't rest. For days and nights, she lay in a fever, asking forgiveness. Finally, her father went for the old curandera, a healer from the village.

The kind old woman came, dressed in black and carrying her herbs and remedies in a small bag. She prayed for Dulcinea and performed a cleansing ceremony to drive away the terror that filled the young girl's heart.

After that, Dulcinea could rest. She recovered slowly, regaining her strength, but her hair had turned white and wrinkles appeared on her face.

Dulcinea was never again seen in the village of Las Pasturas. She would not attend church with her parents; she kept to herself. The girls she had known no longer came to visit, and even Benito could not find the courage to see her.

In the years that followed, the shepherds following their herds across the llano sometimes caught sight of Dulcinea. They saw her crying by the lonely spring at Agua Negra, as if begging for forgiveness. Even the most courageous young men quickly turned away, leaving Dulcinea alone on the vast plain.

Long after she was dead, the people from Las Pasturas claimed they sometimes heard Dulcinea's cry in the wind. Mothers gathered their children close and told them if they disobeyed their parents, the ghost of the crying woman would come to haunt them.

The Three Brothers

Long ago in the village of Chimayó in northern
New Mexico, there lived a man and a woman who
had three sons.

Patricio, the eldest, was headstrong, and he
was not known for telling the truth. When his
father sent him to watch the sheep, he often stole
off to the village pool hall. The parents grew disappointed in this son who squandered away his
time.

Felipe, the middle son, was very lazy. He slept
late in the morning, and when he was sent to weed
the garden, he usually spent the day sleeping
under a tree. There seemed to be no cure for his
laziness.

Ramón, the youngest, was dependable and considerate. He helped his father with the vineyard they owned, raising the best grapes in the region. He was well liked by the neighbors, for they saw he was a hardworking son.

Patricio hated farming, so as soon as he turned fifteen, he decided to leave home. His parents didn't want him to go, but he had made up his mind.

"There is no future here," he told his parents. "If I go to Santa Fe, I can earn a good living."

"But there are temptations on the way," his father warned him. "Many of the young men from our villages have been lost on the road."

"I can take care of myself. I must go," Patricio insisted. "Perhaps there I will find a rich master and become rich myself."

His parents finally relented, and, as was the custom, they gave him their blessing. "God bless you and keep you from evil. Always be kind and help old people. Remember us in your prayers."

Patricio's mother packed provisions for the road, and the young man set off in the direction of Santa Fe. He walked all morning, and at noon he sat beneath a piñon tree to rest and eat his lunch.

While he was eating, he saw a woman coming up the road. Patricio quickly hid his food as she drew near.

"Probably a wandering gypsy," he said. "I'm not going to share my food with her."

The woman stopped in front of Patricio. The blue robe that covered her head fell over her shoulders and down to her feet. She was exceedingly lovely.

"Buenos días, señora," Patricio greeted her. "What is a lady like you doing on this desolate road?"

"I was sent by my son to take care of travelers," she said in a soft voice. "There are many curves and cliffs on this road that are dangerous to young people. There are places of entertainment that promise you everything you desire, only to lead you astray."

"I can take care of myself," replied Patricio. "You, on the other hand, look like you've been working too hard."

"I have been traveling a long time and I am thirsty and hungry."

"I am sorry," Patricio said, "but I have no food or water to share with you." Even as he spoke, he knew he had disobeyed his parents, for they always invited travelers into their home and gave them something to eat and drink. This was the custom of their people.

"Very well," the woman replied. "Where are you going?"

"I am going to Santa Fe to seek my fortune," replied Patricio.

"That road is long and crooked," she said. "There are many temptations. Why not go to work for my son?" she asked.

"Who is your son?"

"He is the master of a large kingdom," she replied. "His

city lies in a peaceful valley, and all the buildings are immaculate and full of light. Follow this straight path and you will find his home. He lives in a shining mansion whose doors are open to all."

"Thank you for the advice," said Patricio.

"Adiós," she said, and continued down the road.

"She is dressed in the finest silk," Patricio muttered, "and her son is rich. I'll go there."

He followed the straight road until he came to the city the woman had described. The green valley surrounding it was the most beautiful Patricio had ever seen. People and animals appeared to live in perfect harmony.

In the center of the valley lay the shining city. Tall spires rose into the clear air. The streets seemed paved with gold, and diamonds glittered everywhere. More than once, Patricio rubbed his eyes, thinking he was dreaming.

When he arrived at the mansion the woman had described, he pinched his arm to reassure himself he was awake. "Truly, I must be dreaming," he said. "I have never seen anything as magnificent as this castle."

Timidly, he knocked on the door, and a young man answered. He was dressed in white, and an aura of light surrounded him.

"Are you the master of this kingdom?" asked Patricio.

"I am," the young man replied.

"I met your mother on the road and gave her food and water," said Patricio. "She said you would reward me."

The young man knew Patricio was lying. Nevertheless, he said, "Thank you for helping her. I will reward you, but first I need you to run an errand for me. My mother has been working for a long time. She must come home to rest. Take my burro and deliver this letter to her. I warn you, on the way you will meet obstacles, and you will be tempted. Take my dog as a companion. Wherever he stops, you will know that is a safe place to rest. But if he barks and pulls you away, don't stop there. That place is evil."

"Very well," Patricio said. Mounted on the burro, he started out, following the dog. He had traveled all day when he came to a dark castle that lay shimmering in the heat like a desert mirage. Music and laughter came from within. People with dark pits for eyes appeared at the door. They called to Patricio to join them.

"Do not waste your time working; here we have entertainment all day and all night," they cried. "Here all your desires will be fulfilled."

"I like that," said Patricio. "This is much more fun than the village pool hall."

He started into the castle, but the dog barked and pulled him away.

"Este perro loco doesn't want me to join the party," Patricio said. "Very well, I'll return later."

He continued on until he came to a river of blood. The dog jumped in, letting Patricio know that it was safe to cross, but Patricio trembled in his boots.

"Too dangerous," he said. "Better to return to the party."

He left the dog and the burro and hurried back to the dark castle. Demons opened the door, and Patricio disappeared within.

Months passed, and Patricio didn't return. Felipe thought his brother must be doing well in Santa Fe, so he decided to join him.

"I will go and live with my brother," he said to his parents. "I am sure he will take care of me, and I will never have to work again. I will leave weeding the garden to Ramón."

His parents protested. They were sure something evil had happened to Patricio, and they did not want to lose another son.

But Felipe was adamant. "I want to share in the good life Patricio has found. Here there is only hard work and going to church. I want a life of ease."

Felipe's parents knew their disobedient son would leave anyway. His mother packed food and water for his journey, and they gave him their blessing.

"God bless you," they said. "Stay away from evil places, and always be kind to old people. Remember us in your prayers."

"Adiós," Felipe said in a hurry. He walked all morning, and when he paused to rest, he saw the same gracious woman Patricio had encountered coming down the road. He quickly hid his provisions so he wouldn't have to share them with her.

"I am hungry," said the woman in blue as she drew near. "Will you share your food with me?"

"I have no food," Felipe replied. He realized he had gone against his parents' teachings.

"Where are you going?" the woman asked.

"I'm looking for my brother. He has found his fortune; I'll never have to work again."

"Your brother has lost his faith," the woman said. "He has gone to live in a dark and frightful world. If you wish to save yourself from a similar fate, you must go to my son's home. He will provide for you."

She began to describe her son's kingdom, and Felipe said, "Yes, yes" to get rid of her.

"Meddlesome woman," he said as she walked away. "What does she mean, Patricio lost his faith? He never had any. But she is dressed in fine silks. Maybe her son is rich. She said he will provide for me. Exactly what I'm looking for!"

So he hurried down the straight road and came to the shining city. Like his brother before him, he was astonished at its magnificence. He had never imagined anything so beautiful.

"This man's mansion is beyond compare," Felipe whispered to himself.

He knocked at the door, and when the young man appeared, Felipe told him he had met his mother on the road. "I gave her food and water and she said you would provide for me."

The young man frowned. He knew Felipe was lying.

"You must be honest if you are to work for me," he said.

"I never lie," replied Felipe.

The master of the mansion had a sure way to test him.

"I provide for all who come to my house," he said. "But first you must deliver this message to my mother. She has been working too hard, and I want her to return home."

He gave Felipe the same instructions he had given Patricio. Felipe saddled the burro and rode away, following the master's dog.

When he came to the dark castle that shimmered like a mirage on fire, he thought he heard his brother's sad voice calling to him: "Do not enter this city of pleasure. Return home and take care of our parents."

Felipe shivered. Through the windows, he caught sight of feverish gambling and drinking.

"This is the easy life I've always wished for," said Felipe. "I bet Patricio just doesn't want to share the good times with me."

He started toward the castle, but the dog nipped at his heels and pulled him away. Try as he might, Felipe couldn't shake the dog loose.

"Okay, dog, I won't go in now. I'll come back later."

He rode on until he came to the river of blood. The dog started forward, but Felipe hesitated. "I will not cross that river," he said, shaking his head. "I'm going back to the castle where I saw the gambling and drinking. I will never lift a finger to work again."

He turned the burro and rode back toward the dark castle.

Many months after Felipe didn't return, Ramón asked his parents' permission to go in search of his brothers.

"No, no, don't go," his mother cried. "Something evil has happened to Patricio and Felipe. We don't want to lose you, too."

"I will return to take care of you," Ramón promised. "This is my home, and I love my work as a farmer. Perhaps my brothers didn't realize that our village is paradise. We work hard, but we have everything we need."

"Very well," his parents agreed. "Go and see if you can find your brothers."

They blessed him for the journey, and his mother packed food and water for him to take.

Ramón walked all morning, and when he stopped to rest, the same woman who had appeared to his brothers came near. Ramón was astounded at her beauty and at the light emanating from her blue robe.

"Good morning, my son," the woman greeted Ramón.

"Buenos días, señora," he greeted her cordially. "I see you have walked a long way. Please rest in the shade of this tree, and I will share my food with you."

Without waiting to be asked, he cleared a place for her

to sit, and he offered her food and water, for this was the custom his parents had taught him.

"Thank you for sharing your food and water with me," she said when she had eaten. "Where are you going?"

"I am looking for my brothers," Ramón answered.

"Go to my son. He will help you." She gave him directions and Ramón thanked her. Then she went on her way.

Ramón lifted his pack of provisions. It had grown heavy, and when he checked it, he found it had been replenished with food and water.

"That woman is surely a saint," he said. He continued on till he came to the magnificent city she had described.

"I am dreaming," said Ramón, "for only paradise could be this beautiful."

He walked to the mansion in the middle of the shining city and knocked. The handsome young man dressed in white came to the door.

"I am looking for my brothers," Ramón said. "Your mother said you can help me. Can you tell me where I might find them?"

"I will tell you, but first I have an errand for you to do. You must deliver this letter to my mother. The people of your region suffer from many hardships, and she goes from village to village, helping them. But she has grown weary, and she must come home to rest. Take my burro and my dog. Trust my dog and follow him. There will be many temptations and obstacles, but if you have faith in me, you will be safe."

"I have faith in you, master," Ramón replied.

He did as he was told, and journeyed till he came to the dark castle surrounded by fire. He heard singing and dancing within, but when he drew near, he saw the people were dancing in pain, not joy.

The dog barked and pulled him away.

"That is not a good place," Ramón said.

He went on until he came to the river of blood. He saw the dog easily start across.

"I can't do that," Ramón cried.

The dog barked, as if asking him to follow.

"My master would not place me in danger," Ramón said, and he and the burro entered the river. The blood turned into sweet, cool water he could drink.

Refreshed, Ramón continued on until he came to two huge mountains that were fighting. The earth shook as the mountains threw boulders and trees at each other. Groaning sounds filled the air, and clouds of dust rose from the angry battle.

Ramón trembled with fear. "How strange," he said. "Two mountains tearing each other apart. Surely I cannot pass."

The dog barked and started forward. Remembering his faith in his master, Ramón urged the burro on and safely passed through the narrow canyon. Not a single rock or tree branch touched him.

Next he came to a dry meadow where many fat sheep grazed. Ramón was puzzled.

"How can the sheep grow fat on such poor grass?" he said.

In a green meadow across the way, a flock of thin sheep grazed.

"Surely I must ask my master the meaning of all this when I return," Ramón said.

Still following the dog, he continued on until he came to a heavenly city. The melodies of pleasing songs filled the air. Angels seemed to hover over the flower gardens and fountains. The dog led Ramón to the door of the mansion where he'd started.

"This is strange," Ramón said in awe. "I have traveled in a circle. This is my master's home. Perhaps it is my faith that has allowed me to return here. But he will be disappointed that I didn't deliver the letter to his mother."

Sadly, he knocked on the door, expecting to be chastised by his master. He was surprised when the woman he had met on the road answered the door.

"Buenas tardes, señora," Ramón said respectfully. "I have a message from your son. But I have come too late, for I see you have returned home."

"You are not late," answered the gracious woman in blue. "We have been waiting for you. You shared your food and water with me. You may enter."

She led him into the mansion, and Ramón's heart beat with joy. He had never seen anything so beautiful. The melody in the air filled him with peace. In the gardens, flowers grew so profusely they created dazzling rainbows. Trees lined the paths, and everywhere people moved and talked with great joy. Ramón had never known such contentment.

The woman led him to a table laden with many savory dishes. He enjoyed the most delicious meal he had ever eaten. Then she took him to a luxurious room where he could rest. A weary Ramón was soon asleep.

The next morning, he heard the woman calling him at the door. "Wake up, Ramón. My son is here to greet you."

Ramón stretched. His sleep had been profound and comfortable, but now it was time to rise and meet his master. He jumped out of bed.

"Good morning, Ramón," said the master, entering the room. "I see you have had a good rest."

"It was a restful and peaceful sleep. I dreamed I was with my father and mother and we were happy."

"Soon you will be reunited with your parents," said the woman.

"You are a good son and a faithful worker," the master added. "You have followed my instructions. Now you may wish for anything you desire."

"I desire no reward," Ramón answered. "But I would like to know about my brothers."

"Your brothers went to the city where all their desires

could be fulfilled," the master replied. "That city is hell, and they will spend eternity there."

Ramón grew very sad. Tears filled his eyes and ran down his cheeks.

"Do not cry," said the master, comforting Ramón. "Each person chooses his own path."

"That is what my father always said," Ramón replied, accepting the fate of his brothers. "As for me, I have seen so many wondrous things. I knew I could cross the river of blood because I had faith in you."

"That is true," the master replied. "The river water has renewed you. You are a new person."

"But what do the two angry mountains mean?"

"Those are two angry neighbors who hate each other. They spend their time heaping insults on each other instead of living in peace."

"Why were the sheep fat even when the grass was dry?"

"That is my flock, and though they have a meager pasture, they thrive and are content because they have faith in me."

"And the thin sheep?"

"Those are people who have lost their faith. No matter how green the pasture, they remain poor in spirit."

"And this mansion?"

"This is heaven."

Ramón was overjoyed. By following his master's instructions, he had come to visit heaven.

"And you, master, you must be—"

"I am the Lord, and you are one of my flock. You have given food and water to the hungry, and you could pass through obstacles because of your faith in me. Now you must return to your parents and help them in their old age."

Ramón thanked the Lord for everything. He returned home and told his parents about his adventures, and what had happened to his brothers.

Thereafter, Ramón lived a good life in the village of his birth. He worked hard, helping his parents care for their small farm. As he grew older, he became known as one of the most honest and generous men in the region, and he prospered.

Later, he married his childhood sweetheart, and when his children were growing up, he often told them of his adventures. He told them his brothers had chosen the wrong path in life, and that they had gone to live in hell. And he told them that if they had faith in their hearts, they could overcome every obstacle.

Doña Sebastiana

Baltazar, the woodcutter, lived in the village of Arroyo Seco at the foot of Taos Mountain. He earned his living by cutting firewood in the forests and selling it in the village.

Each morning, he took his burro up the mountain where he cut dead pine trees and aspen. Then he made his way down the perilous road to sell the wood to housewives. When he made a sale, he went to the village store and bought meat and potatoes for his family. When he didn't sell the wood, he led his burro back to his adobe home by the stream.

One evening, Baltazar's wife and ten children saw him returning with the wood still piled on the burro's back. This summer, the housewives had plenty of wood for cooking, so Baltazar hadn't sold a load in a week. All knew their supper would consist of corn gruel and yesterday's stale tortillas.

"No luck today," Baltazar said as he drew near.

"Don't worry, viejo," said his understanding wife. "Maybe tomorrow you'll have better luck."

"Sí, there's always tomorrow," Baltazar replied. His wife and children didn't seem to mind the corn gruel, but after eating it three meals a day for the past week, he had grown very tired of it.

"Unload the burro and let it eat grass along the stream," he told his eldest son. "I'm going to visit my compadre Felipe."

"Sí, Papá," the boy answered, and went off to do his father's bidding.

Baltazar's wife knew that when her husband went off to visit Felipe, the compadre who long ago had been best man at their wedding, they probably would have a few cups of wine. The two old friends liked to sit and talk in the cool summer evenings, so Baltazar wouldn't be home till late.

Baltazar's wife understood that the life of a woodcutter wasn't easy, so she sighed and went in to prepare a supper of corn gruel for herself and her children.

Baltazar walked down the dirt road to his compadre's house, and the two sat visiting till it was dark. By the time Baltazar started for home, a full moon had come over Taos

Mountain, lighting the path. Baltazar always felt happy after visiting with his compadre, but the good feeling didn't assuage the growling hunger in his stomach.

He knew only a bowl of cold corn gruel awaited him at home. He sighed and spoke to the moon. "Luna, you are so lucky. You are full and fat and happy. I am happy, but thin and hungry."

Passing by his neighbors' home, he saw that one of the hens had been left out of the henhouse when it was locked for the night. The poor hen ran up and down the fence, clucking in fear.

"Pobre gallina," Baltazar said. "If someone doesn't put you in the henhouse, an owl or a coyote will surely get you."

He grabbed the hen, with the thought of putting it into the coop. The hen grew quiet in his arms. Baltazar looked around. His neighbors' home was dark; everyone was asleep.

Then Baltazar's hunger overcame his honesty. He hadn't had a good meal in a week.

"My neighbor has many chickens," Baltazar said. "He surely won't miss one. So I will borrow it."

With the chicken under his arm, he made his way up the mountainside to a clearing. There he made a fire, killed and plucked the thin hen, and put it on a spit to roast. As the aroma of the baking chicken filled the air, Baltazar felt his stomach growl.

For a moment, he thought of his family. Maybe he should share the chicken with them. No, he thought, they are asleep. Why bother them? Besides, the chicken was so small, it hardly made a meal for one person.

He removed the chicken from the spit and was about to take his first bite when he heard someone coming.

God help me! he thought. Even here I can't be left alone to enjoy myself. Well, whoever it is, I'm not going to invite him to eat!

A tall stranger approached the fire. He was dressed in a flowing white robe, and an aura of light surrounded him.

"How do you do, my friend," said the noble stranger.

"Buenas noches," Baltazar responded. "Who are you?"

"I am the Lord," the man answered. "I have been traveling all day and I am hungry. Will you invite me to eat with you?"

Baltazar looked at the small chicken. Again his stomach growled. If He is the Lord, surely He can find food somewhere else, Baltazar thought. Besides, He hasn't been too good to me lately. It is His fault I haven't been able to sell my wood and eat a decent meal. I must think of an excuse.

"No," he finally said. "I don't think I'll invite you to share my meal, and I'll tell you why. If you were watching over me, you would make sure I can sell my wood. You neglect the poor. You give everything to the rich. You don't treat us equally."

The Lord went away, looking sad. Baltazar was satisfied that someone as powerful as the Lord hadn't given him an argument. Again he held the chicken up, ready to eat, when he heard the sound of another person approaching.

The woman who drew near the fire was beautiful beyond description. She wore a blue robe, and rays of light seemed to emanate from her.

"Good evening, my friend," said the woman.

"Buenas noches, señora," the woodcutter replied. "And who might you be?"

"I am the Virgin Mary," the woman answered. "I have been traveling all day and I am hungry. Will you share your food with me?"

Baltazar scratched his beard and looked at the small chicken. If he gave half away, there would be hardly any bites left for himself. His stomach growled, reminding him of the hunger he had suffered all week. There must be an excuse he could use to satisfy the Virgin Mary.

"No," he finally said. "I am not going to share my food with you, and I'll tell you why. I think your son neglects the poor. Since you are the mother of Jesus, you should intercede for us to ask Him to make us all equal. Either we should all be rich or we should all be poor. The way it is now, He makes some very rich and some very poor, and, unfortunately, I am one of the poor ones. For that reason, I'm not going to share my chicken with you."

The Virgin Mary turned and left without a word.

"Good," Baltazar said. "She didn't argue with me."

He opened his mouth to bite into the chicken, when he heard someone else on the mountain path. When Baltazar looked up, he saw it was Doña Sebastiana, Death herself, who approached the fire. Her skeleton was thinly clothed in rags, and her dark eye pits made Baltazar shiver.

Oh no, Baltazar thought, my time has come. Maybe the Lord and the Virgin Mary have sent Death to get even with me for not sharing my food.

He closed his eyes and began to whisper a prayer. But Death did not string an arrow on the bow she carried. Instead, she greeted him.

"How goes it, friend?" Doña Sebastiana asked.

"Buenas noches," the woodcutter answered, trembling at the sight of the old hag. "Who are you?" he asked.

"I am la Muerte," Doña Sebastiana answered. "I have been traveling all day and I am hungry. Will you share your meal with me?"

"Yes, you do *look* hungry!" Baltazar said, eyeing the skeleton in front of him.

Maybe if I share my chicken with Doña Sebastiana she won't take me, he thought.

"Of course you're welcome to share my meal," Baltazar said, motioning to a tree stump where Death might sit. "And I'll tell you why. You treat us all equally. You don't play favorites with the wealthy because of their money, nor with the beautiful because of their beauty. Rich or poor, beautiful or ugly, old or young, you treat us all equally. Sit down and share my food."

Still shivering at the sight of Death, Baltazar tore the

chicken apart and offered Doña Sebastiana half. After they had finished eating the roasted chicken, Doña Sebastiana seemed satisfied.

"You are wise to share your meal with me," she said. "I will reward you. Ask for any favor you desire and it will be granted."

"Señora," Baltazar said in his most humble voice, "I just wish I could sell my firewood so I can feed my family."

"I will help you feed your family," Death answered. "I am going to grant you a special power. You are to become a curandero, a healer. You will be able to cure all kinds of sickness, and people will reward you with food."

"Thank you, señora," Baltazar replied.

"However, there is one time when you must not cure a sick person."

"When is that, señora?"

"If you go to a patient's bed and see me standing at the head of it, don't cure that person, regardless of what his relatives will pay or promise you. That person has no remedy but to die. Do you understand?"

"Yes I do, señora. If you are at the head of the bed, I must *not* cure the person."

"But if you see me at the patient's feet, then go ahead and cure him. Use prayers, holy water, and herbs to help the sick. I assure you your patients will get well."

Then Death got on her creaking wooden cart and disappeared into the night. When she had gone, a very frightened

Baltazar raced down the mountain. Once he tripped and fell and came within inches of rolling off the side of the cliff. Bruised and scratched, he hurried home, climbed into bed, and lay trembling for a long time.

The next morning, he got up late, battered but happy to be alive. He knew no one would believe his story, so he said nothing to his wife. Besides, she had her own story to tell as she served his breakfast of corn gruel.

Cruz Trujillo, a neighbor at the Indian pueblo, had fallen from a horse. He was near death.

"Toña is my best friend," Baltazar's wife said. "I will bake some corn bread and take it to her. They will need firewood."

"Yes, I will take them a load of firewood."

It was the custom of the neighbors of Arroyo Seco to help one another in time of need, so as soon as the corn bread was ready, Baltazar and his wife went to the pueblo.

When Baltazar walked into the room where the semiconscious Cruz lay, a strange feeling came over him. Without a word, he walked up to the prone man and began to massage him. Baltazar's wife and Toña were surprised but said nothing.

After a while, Baltazar said, "He is lucky; there are no broken bones." He made a few adjustments of the compacted bones, and when he was done, Cruz opened his eyes.

"Gracias, compadre" were his first words. Those in the room were astounded. Baltazar had instantly cured Cruz.

The news traveled like a forest fire though the Indian

pueblos, then to the Hispanic villages of the Río Grande valley. Everywhere, the message was whispered: "Baltazar the woodcutter is a curandero. He has the power to heal any sickness!"

Sick people flocked to see Baltazar, and he traveled to many villages, practicing his healing craft. Because most of the people he cured were poor, they paid him with what they had at home. If a man raised corn, Baltazar would go home with his burro loaded with corn. Some would give him a side of beef or a cured ham. Women offered eggs from the hens they raised.

Baltazar's fame spread, and his family prospered. They ate regularly every day and glowed with good health. And Baltazar kept Death's commandment. He never attempted a cure if he saw the figure of Death, which only he could see, at the head of a sick person's bed.

One afternoon, Baltazar's wife spoke to him. "We are doing well, viejo. Look at how happy and healthy our children are. And you are famous. Whoever gave you this gift of healing has done you a great favor."

"Yes," Baltazar said, frowning. "I heal people when no one else can help them. But they pay me with what they raise, not money. Doctors and lawyers and undertakers get paid with gold coins, but I get paid with chickens and eggs."

"The poor don't have gold," his wife reminded him. "You provide very well for your family. Remember the days of hunger when you were a woodcutter. Thank the saints for your gift."

Baltazar didn't thank the saints. He felt Doña Sebastiana had cheated him. Yes, she had given him a gift, but it didn't make him any money. He should have asked for a lost fortune. That way, he could have built a big house like a rico. Then he could have sat all day on his porch and done nothing.

The next day, when Baltazar was readying his burro for a trip to Santa Fe, his wife came running. "Don Mateo has sent for you!" she cried, out of breath. "His daughter is very sick!"

Don Mateo was the richest man in Arroyo Hondo, so Baltazar got on his burro and rode along the side of the cliff and down into the valley. Don Mateo and his family lived in a grand house by the curve of the road. A servant led Baltazar into the sala, a spacious living room, where Don Mateo was waiting.

"Baltazar," he said, "I have heard you are a great curandero. For weeks, my daughter has been ill. She runs a high fever and wastes away. I have taken her to the doctors at Taos and Santa Fe, but they say there is nothing they can do. I beg you to save her life."

He led Baltazar into his daughter's room. It was a room fit for a queen, Baltazar thought, noting the fine rugs on the floor and the lace curtains on the windows. The girl's mother sat nearby, ever attentive to her daughter, who lay on the bed in a coma.

As Baltazar approached the girl, he saw the figure of Death standing at the head of the bed. Baltazar shivered and pulled back.

"I . . . I can't," he stammered.

Don Mateo grabbed his arm. "What do you mean you can't! We have been told you perform miracles! You must try something!"

Baltazar didn't have the nerve to tell the distraught father his daughter was dying.

"You must do something!" Don Mateo's wife said. "She is our only daughter."

Baltazar shook his head. He had made a bargain with Death not to interfere under such circumstances.

"I will pay you handsomely!" Don Mateo said. "Look!" He opened a chest, and hundreds of gold coins glittered. "It is our family fortune, but it is yours if you cure our daughter."

Baltazar picked up the gold coins and let them trickle through his fingers. His eyes gleamed. I would be the richest man in Río Arriba, he thought. Yes, for this fortune, I would cheat Death.

"Very well," he said, turning to Don Mateo. "I will cure your daughter. Please leave the room."

Don Mateo took one final look at his daughter; then he took his wife's hand and they left the room.

Baltazar turned and approached Doña Sebastiana.

"You cannot save her!" Death warned, stringing an arrow to her bow. But before she could point it at the girl, Baltazar grabbed her. He spun Death around so fast, she grew dizzy. Then he pushed her to the foot of the bed.

"There!" he cried. "The girl does not die!"

"You win this time, my friend," Death said, and stalked angrily out of the room.

At that moment, the girl sat up in her bed and called for her mother. Her parents came rushing in and found her completely cured. The healer had performed another miracle.

"We are thankful you have cured our daughter," Don Mateo said. "I will have my servants load the bags of gold coins on your burro."

As Baltazar rode home that night, a furious storm came up. Lightning filled the sky and thunder shook the earth. Rain slashed in sheets to the ground, making the footing along the cliff dangerous.

No matter, Baltazar thought. His burro was loaded with gold. Never again would he have to raise his finger to work. He would build a big house and live like a rich man the rest of his life. He would never eat corn gruel again.

Suddenly, the figure of Death loomed before him, an arrow from her bow aimed at Baltazar.

"You broke your promise," Doña Sebastiana said angrily. "Now you must pay me with your life."

The burro, too, felt the presence of Death as lightning illuminated the dreadful figure. In terror, it reared up and lost its footing on the muddy road. Then it went tumbling over the side of the cliff, taking Baltazar to his death.

He who had cheated Death could not do so this time. She had come too swiftly. The next day when Baltazar's family found his body, they placed a small cross by the side of the road where he had died. The gold was never found.

The Shepherd Who Knew the Language of Animals

Abel lived with his mother in the village of Anton Chico, a farming community on the banks of the Río Pecos in central New Mexico. When Abel was seven, his father had died, so Abel grew up taking care of the family's small plot of land near the river. Together, mother and son raised enough vegetables to trade for the things they needed at the village store.

One spring, it did not rain, and the river was almost dry. Only hardy catfish and carp survived in the shallow pools that were left. The young plants in Abel's garden withered and died. Abel knew they would not have a vegetable crop, and though he was only fourteen, it was up to him to provide for himself and his mother.

"I must go and look for work," he said to her one day.

"What kind of work could you find?" she asked.

"I was at the store yesterday, and Don Nicanor told me he needs a shepherd to take care of a flock of sheep. He pays a dollar a week. I will make enough money to see us through the winter."

His mother reluctantly agreed. She packed a knapsack with provisions: beans, red chile, corn, lard, and jerky. She included a small bag of flour so Abel could make tortillas. She also packed a change of clothes.

Before he left, Abel went to see Adelina, a girl in the village. That past winter, he had helped her father milk his few cows. Adelina was friendly and easy to talk to, and Abel had grown fond of the dark-haired girl. Each night, after the milking was done, she would give him milk and cheese to take home.

Abel felt very grown-up as he explained where he was going.

"I'm going to take care of Don Nicanor's sheep this summer. I would like to see you when I return."

"And I would like to see you," she replied. "Let me give you something to remember me by."

She cut a wisp of her dark hair and put it in the locket around her neck. She gave him the locket and kissed his cheek.

"I pray you will be safe."

Abel blushed. How lucky he was. He had a man's job,

and the lovely Adelina would wait for his return.

"Adiós," he stammered. "I will think of you."

Then Abel whistled to his dog, Flojo, and off he went to take care of the sheep.

The following day, he drove the flock of sheep toward La Mesa Parda. He made a camp at the foot of the flat tableland. All day, he and Flojo followed the sheep as they browsed the dry grass, and at sunset he drove them back to the camp.

He prepared his supper of beans, corn, and jerky, seasoned with the chile his mother had sent. He wrapped the food in a tortilla and ate. He fed his dog some jerky and three tortillas, which the hungry Flojo gobbled down.

After supper, he rested and looked up at the bright sweep of the Milky Way.

"How lucky we are," he said to Flojo. "We have work and the beauty of nature to keep us company. When I return in the fall, I will have money for my mother and enough to buy Adelina a gold ring."

He touched the locket she had given him and fell into a peaceful sleep.

At night, the coyotes cried in the hills, but Abel slept soundly. He knew Flojo wouldn't allow the coyotes to come near the sheep.

Weeks passed, and one day when Abel was leading the flock to graze, he saw an ominous storm brewing. The flat mesa grew dark as a menacing cloud descended. It did not rain, but lightning and thunder filled the sky.

Abel took cover beneath a piñon tree. Lightning bolts thundered around him, and one set the dry grass on fire. A strong wind fanned the flames, and soon a roaring prairie fire swept across the arid land.

As Abel ran to see if any of his sheep were in the path of the flames, he heard a hissing sound, and he came upon a strange sight. Wrapped around the branches of a juniper tree was a small snake. It had climbed the tree to escape, but now the tongues of fire reached upward and the snake cried for help.

Abel quickly picked up a long stick and held it so the snake was able to slither down and escape the fire. When it was safe, the snake wrapped itself around the boy's arm. Startled, Abel tried to shake it loose, but he couldn't. The snake clung tightly to his arm. Flojo barked loudly, but even that didn't frighten it.

Then the snake spoke to Abel.

"Don't be frightened, my young savior. I am grateful to you for saving my life. To show my gratitude, I will take you to my mother, and she will reward you handsomely."

"Who is your mother and where does she live?" asked a startled Abel.

"My mother is a queen snake and she lives in a cave at the foot of the mesa," the snake answered. "Follow me and I will show you."

Abel followed the snake until they came to a large cave. At the entrance of the cave, the little snake stopped and again spoke to Abel. "My mother will offer you money as a reward for saving my life, but don't accept it. Ask instead for the gift of understanding the language of animals. That will serve you far better than all the money in the world."

Abel was still so astounded that all he could do was nod.

First he turned to see if his sheep were safe. The prairie fire had skirted the flock and the sheep grazed contentedly near the camp.

"Go take care of the sheep," Abel told his dog. Flojo barked and ran to watch over them.

Then Abel entered the cave and followed the snake into a dark chamber. There was just enough light from the entrance to reveal the mother snake, a huge creature coiled in quiet dignity.

Abel shivered with fright. He had never seen such a large snake. He had heard shepherds tell stories about a giant snake who lived in Mesa Parda, but no one had ever seen it. Now Abel knew the stories were true.

"Mother of all the snakes," the small snake said respectfully, "I have brought with me a young shepherd who has saved my life. I was surrounded by a fire and I climbed a tree to escape, but still the flames reached up to burn me. I called for help and this young shepherd came to my rescue. Now I have brought him here so you might repay his kindness."

Abel stood trembling before the giant glistening snake. He held his breath as he looked into her eyes and waited for her to speak.

"Thank you for saving my daughter's life," said the mother snake. "If you had not rescued her, she would have perished in the fire. Now, ask for anything you want and it shall be yours."

"The only thing I desire in this world is the gift of understanding the language of animals," answered Abel.

"That can't be!" the giant snake hissed, and Abel almost fell backward from the furious blast. "Ask for money and I will give it to you! Ask me for a kingdom and it will be yours!"

Abel composed himself and glanced at the small snake. It was true! If the mother snake wouldn't grant him this request, then the gift must be very valuable.

"I don't want money," Abel insisted. "I want to understand the animals. If you can't give me that as a reward, then I don't want anything."

He turned to leave, but the mother snake called him back.

"Very well," she said, "I will give you what you desire. I refused at first because it is a very powerful gift. One must be very wise and brave to receive it. From your deed, I know you are brave, and by your words, I know you are wise, so I will grant it to you."

"I am willing to accept the responsibility," said Abel.

"Open your mouth so that I can touch your tongue with mine," the snake commanded.

Abel shuddered. He saw the forked tongue of the snake

flick out, red and glistening in the near dark. His knees trembled, but he was determined to go ahead. He opened his mouth and felt the warm tongue of the snake touch his own tongue. It burned as if on fire, and for a moment he wondered if he had done the right thing.

"Now you possess the power to understand the speech of all the animals," the mother of all the snakes said. "But I must warn you of one thing. You must never tell anyone this secret, because if you do, you will die! Now go."

Abel left the cave, shaking like a cottonwood leaf in a storm. He stumbled toward the camp and came upon a pack of coyotes.

"Here comes the shepherd!" the father coyote called to the others. "We can't steal one of his lambs today." They ran off.

Abel was astounded. He had actually heard the coyote speak. When he got over his surprise, he threw his hat in the air and leapt with joy. He was amazed at his newfound power.

"I understand the coyote's language!" he shouted.

He neared his flock in time to hear the conversation the sheep were having.

"Here comes our careless shepherd," said a large ram. "He left us alone for so long, it would serve him right if a coyote or wolf had eaten us all."

"It wouldn't serve *us* right," another sheep answered, and they laughed and went on gossiping as they grazed.

Abel understood everything they said. All around him, the animals were talking. Two crows on a nearby tree discussed where to eat. Jackrabbits called to one another as they ran races, and even the chipmunks chattered about family affairs.

Abel had entered a world nobody else knew. He sat listening to the conversations of the animals, feeling thankful for this wonderful gift that had been granted to him. He had never before realized that the animals could speak so knowingly about the matters of life.

The following morning, he rose early, eager to listen to the animals discuss their concerns.

"Adelina and my mother will never believe me," he said to Flojo.

Then he remembered the giant serpent's admonition: *You must never tell anyone this secret, because if you do, you will die!*

That night, Abel hardly slept. He lay awake and thought about his special gift, and the fact that he couldn't tell anyone about it.

The next day, as a weary Abel sat under a piñon tree watching his flock, two large crows alighted on the branches overhead. Not knowing he could understand their language, they began to talk about him.

"Just look at that lazy shepherd; he lies in the shade of the tree all day while his dog watches the sheep. What a life he leads!"

"Poor man," the other crow answered, "if only he knew that many years ago a gang of bandits buried a treasure at the very spot where he sits. The gold buried there would make him the richest man in New Mexico."

Abel immediately sat up and began to dig. He dug hard and eagerly, not minding that he scraped his fingers. A few feet below the surface he found a large, flat stone, and he used a stick to dig around it. When he lifted the stone, he uncovered an old copper-plated trunk. He pried open the lid with his knife. It was full of gold coins!

"A fortune!" he cried. "I found a fortune!"

He filled his pockets with coins, then buried the trunk again and carefully covered up all signs of his digging.

He and Flojo hurriedly drove the flock to Don Nicanor's ranch.

"I am sorry, but I cannot care for your sheep anymore," Abel told his employer.

"I should have known better than to trust a lazy boy!" Don Nicanor responded angrily. "Get off my ranch and never come back!"

Several of the workers heard him threaten Abel, who could only turn away and hurry home with Flojo at his side.

When he arrived home, his mother greeted him at the door.

"¡Mi hijo!" she cried with joy. "I'm so glad to see you. Gracias a Dios," she said, embracing Abel.

"And I'm glad to see you, Mamá," said Abel.

"But I didn't expect you until the end of summer. Are you all right?"

"Oh yes," Abel replied, closing the door tightly behind him and drawing the curtains.

"What is it?" she asked, startled by his actions.

"Come here," he whispered, and emptied his pockets on the table.

"Gold!" she cried. "But where did you get so much money? Surely Don Nicanor didn't pay you all this. Did you steal it?"

"No, I didn't steal it, but I can't tell you how I came upon it. It's ours. Now go to the store and buy anything your heart desires. As for me, I'm going to buy the palomino Don Felipe has for sale. I will never again travel on foot like a shepherd. And I'm going to buy a gold ring for Adelina."

Abel's mother immediately went to the store. They had always been poor and couldn't afford meat, but now she bought the biggest roast the storekeeper had on hand. She bought cakes and fruit and candy, and she paid with a gold coin.

The surprised storekeeper bit the coin. It was real gold. Other women in the store were equally surprised. This poor widow who could barely afford beans and potatoes was now buying meat and sweet desserts.

The women left the store whispering, "Her son has stolen the money."

In the meantime, Abel went off to buy the beautiful

palomino and the ring. Those who saw him began to gossip. Soon the whole village knew of Abel's fortune.

That same afternoon, Don Nicanor was found dead on his ranch. When the sheriff came to investigate, some of the ranch hands told him they had seen Don Nicanor arguing with Abel. A few said maybe Abel had killed him for his money.

But the sheriff found no evidence to arrest Abel. That did not stop the people from suspecting Abel and spreading the rumor that he was a murderer.

That evening, Abel went to call on Adelina. By now, everyone knew about Abel's fortune. Adelina's parents invited Abel inside. They left the room and huddled behind the kitchen door to overhear what he was going to say to their daughter.

"I have come to ask you to marry me," Abel said. "If you give me a pumpkin, I will know you do not accept my proposal."

"I have always loved you," the kindhearted Adelina replied. "But everyone is asking how you came upon your newfound wealth. I will not marry a thief. You must tell me how you made your fortune."

A frown crossed Abel's face. "I will keep no secret from you but this one. I cannot tell you how I found my fortune. I can tell you that I am not a thief or a murderer."

"I believe you," Adelina said. "I will marry you."

At that moment, her eager parents pressed their ears so

close to the door that it flew open and they fell into the room. Adelina and Abel jumped up. Soon all were laughing. The parents told Abel they accepted him as their son-in-law.

A few days later, Abel bought a burro and two sacks. He told his mother he would soon return. He traveled to the place of the buried treasure, dug out the trunk, and filled the two sacks with the gold coins. He loaded them on the burro, covered the hole, and returned home.

When he arrived home, his mother almost fainted at the sight of so much gold.

"We must say nothing about this," Abel warned her. "Help me dig a hole here in the kitchen floor."

They dug a deep hole and buried the gold; then Abel erased all signs of the hiding place. Shortly thereafter, he began to buy land, until his ranch was the largest in the county. He went to Dilia, Colonias, and to the ranches around Santa Rosa to buy flocks of sheep and herds of cattle. He had quickly become the richest man in the county.

During that time, he courted Adelina, bestowing wonderful gifts on her and her family. A year later, they were married in the church at Anton Chico, and Abel threw the biggest wedding feast anyone could remember.

A few months after they were married, Abel and Adelina rode out to the pastureland to check on the livestock. He was riding his palomino and Adelina, who was now pregnant, followed slowly behind on her mare. Abel's horse pranced and danced smartly, urging the mare to race, but the mare refused and kept her slow pace.

The horse spoke to the mare: "Why are you so slow? Why don't you hurry and keep up with me?"

"Why do you think?" the mare answered. "I carry more weight. There are three of us, and only two of you!"

Abel, who had overheard their conversation, thought the mare's answer was clever, and he began to laugh. Adelina thought he was laughing at her.

"What are you laughing at?" she asked. "I don't see anything funny!"

Abel couldn't tell her what the mare had said, so he grew quiet. He knew that he couldn't reveal his secret, even to his wife. Instead of forgetting the incident, she kept after him to tell her why he had laughed.

"You are so secretive," she said. "Everyone talks about you."

"Let them gossip," Abel replied. "It doesn't hurt me."

"But it hurts me," his wife retorted.

"How?"

"People still want to know how you acquired your fortune. You know that Don Nicanor died the same day you came home a rich man. Some say you killed him and stole his money."

Abel grew angry. "I told you the day I proposed to you that I am not a thief or a murderer. Those who knew Don

Nicanor know the old man died of a heart attack. That's why the sheriff didn't arrest me."

"Then how did you get your fortune?" she asked.

"Very well, I'll tell you. One day when I was sheep-herding, I overheard two crows—" Abel stopped. A chill ran through him even though the day was warm. He couldn't tell her! He couldn't tell anyone!

"Overheard two crows?" his wife questioned. "What do you mean?"

"It's nothing."

"You mean you won't tell me? I'm your wife. I deserve to know. It's not fair for me to have to live with all the gossip! If you don't tell me, I'll know you don't love me anymore!"

With that, she turned her mare and rode back to the house, and for weeks after the argument, she wouldn't speak to him. She had decided it wasn't fair for her husband to keep the secret of his fortune from her. Of course she didn't know that if he revealed it, he would die.

Abel grew very sad. He couldn't eat or sleep, and he spent his days riding alone. He loved Adelina so much, he couldn't bear to live with her silence.

One day, Abel rode out on the range, trying to decide what to tell his wife. Flojo ran alongside, every once in a while giving chase to rabbits.

Flojo never caught a rabbit, because as soon as one saw

him, he called to the others, "Run for the hole. Here comes the Flojo dog!"

Abel stopped to wait for Flojo, and while he waited, he spied a snake on the trail. It was the same snake he had saved from the fire.

"Good friend Abel," the snake said in greeting. "How goes it?"

"Not well," Abel said. He told the snake his predicament.

"What have you decided?" asked the snake.

"Tonight I will tell my wife how I came into my fortune. I will not keep the secret from her."

"You will die," the snake reminded him.

"Yes," Abel said sadly. "But I love her so much, I must do it."

"Wait until tomorrow," the snake said. "Secrets are better shared in the light of morning, when the day is new. That way, they don't bother your sleep."

"I will do as you say," Abel told the snake. "Tell your mother that I have had great joy in knowing the language of animals. At first, I wanted to be a rich man, but now that I am rich, I realize the greatest gift is to understand the creatures of the earth."

"As my mother said, you *are* a wise man," the snake said, and slithered toward Mesa Parda.

That night while Adelina slept, she had a dark and ominous dream. She was walking in the llano with her husband when she fell into a cavern. "Help me!" she cried, but there was no response.

She walked deeper into the cave, until she came upon a giant mother snake. Adelina cringed in fear, sure the snake would eat her.

"Do not be fearful," the snake said. "I have come into your dream to tell you something very important. In every person's past, there are secrets. Sometimes the secrets are so close to your heart that you cannot share them with anyone else."

"I know," replied Adelina, realizing the giant snake spoke with great wisdom.

"What is your secret?"

"I will never tell my husband that before we were married I fell in love with a young rancher from Villanueva. I had promised Abel I'd wait for him, but this young man swept me off my feet. I told him I loved him. Nothing happened between us, and in a few days he rode away. I tell my husband all my secrets, but I can't tell him I let my emotions stray that summer. I love my husband, and there is no need to awaken his jealousy."

As she said that, the mother snake disappeared, and Adelina heard a voice. It was Abel calling. He had found the cave, and now he reached down and pulled her out of the cavern.

Adelina awoke in a start. She was trembling from the vivid dream. The giant serpent had spoken to her, and

Adelina had learned a lesson from the dream. She, too, had a secret she couldn't reveal to Abel.

She got up, threw her gown around her, and hurried to the kitchen, where she found a very dejected Abel drinking a cup of coffee.

He looked at her and said, "I have something to tell you."

She went to him and stroked his cheek. "Before you speak, let me say something. Tonight I learned that secrets belong to the person who owns them. I beg you not to tell me how you earned your fortune. It is your business, and it is not time for you to reveal it."

Abel was overcome with joy. He jumped up and put his arms around his wife. "Thank you, my love. I will keep no other secret from you. And this one I will reveal on the day I die."

"Until then," Adelina said, "let us be content that our love is our greatest fortune."

Outside on the patio, Flojo had overheard the conversation. He barked with joy.

"Sounds like your dog is speaking to you," said Adelina, winking.

"Yes," said Abel, returning her smile. "All the animals speak to us, if we only listen."

The Fountain of Youth

Rolando de Espada lived in a small village in Extremadura, Spain. His family was large and extremely poor. Rolando's mother had died when he was six, so he grew up under the harsh tutelage of his brothers. From the time he could remember, Rolando had worked from sunup to sunset in his father's olive orchards.

Rolando's father knew his son worked hard, and one day he drew him aside and spoke to him.

"My son, there is only poverty in our village. My orchards will be inherited by your older brothers. What are you to do?"

"Do not worry, Father," Rolando replied. "I am fifteen, and it is time for me to go out into the world. If you will let me take the old mare, I will travel to the king's court and seek my fortune there."

As a child, Rolando had dreamed of seeking fame and adventure in foreign lands. The village schoolmaster had often told his handful of students fabulous stories of the New World. He described the Aztec empire captured by the Spaniards and the fabulous wealth in gold and jade that had been taken from those tribes. He related old fables of a land in the Americas ruled by the Amazons, whose queen was Calafia.

But the most intriguing story he told was that of a Fountain of Youth. Anyone who drank from its water was assured immortality. That tale made a deep impression on Rolando. What if his mother had had water from that fountain? Then she would not have died so young.

The stories instilled an urge for adventure in Rolando. He often lingered in the plaza, practicing mock sword fights with the other boys. When they rested in the shade of the church, they talked about being knights in the service of the king.

"Someday I will go to the New World," Rolando boasted. "I will bring back enough gold to pave the streets of our village."

The other boys laughed. As the story spread throughout the village, the older people also laughed when they saw Rolando.

But Rolando was undaunted. That spring when his

brothers went to work in the olive orchards, Rolando saddled his father's old swaybacked mare and rode out of the village.

Alas, he was not greeted as a knight in the king's court. He had no sword, only a shepherd's staff, and he wore no armor. The mare got him as far as the court, then expired from the journey. Rolando went to work as a page, serving the lords and ladies who filled the great hall each day and waited on the king.

Rolando listened and paid attention to the comings and goings of the nobles. The Spaniards had just defeated the Moors and driven them out of Spain. A few decades earlier, a man named Columbus had discovered a New World by sailing west. As his schoolmaster had described, riches were pouring in from the conquest of Mexico. The New World adventures Rolando heard about in court seemed even more exciting than his schoolmaster's tales.

He dreamed of going to the New World. He yearned for adventure. Most of all, he wanted to return to his village a rich man.

One day at court, Rolando heard the king complaining.

"My conquistadores have brought back much gold from the Americas," the king said. "But what good is gold if I cannot live forever to enjoy it? What if a man could live forever?"

"Impossible." The lords and ladies-in-waiting sighed.

"But I have heard stories from those who have been in

the New World. They say there is a Fountain of Youth in the land of the Amazons. According to the stories the natives tell, the spring gushes from a fountain guarded by a genie. One drink of that water and a person will live forever."

Rolando perked up his ears. He, too, had heard the stories about the adventurers who sought the Fountain of Youth.

"I would knight the man who found that fountain and brought me a drink of its water," the king continued. "And I would give my eldest daughter in marriage to such a man."

The lords and ladies oohed and aahed. The king had made a royal offer, a challenge. Several knights instantly stepped forward.

"Let me go, Your Royal Highness," they said in unison.

The offer was too much for Rolando to resist. He stepped forward and blurted, "I will find the Fountain of Youth, Your Majesty."

Everyone turned to look at the brash young page. A ripple of uneasy laughter spread through the audience. How dare this servant address the king?

But something in Rolando's voice drew the king's attention. He looked into the young man's eyes and saw desire burning there.

"Step forward." The king motioned. "What is your name, young man?"

"Rolando de Espada, at your service, Your Most Royal Majesty."

"What makes you think you can find the Fountain of Youth, Rolando?"

"I will find it or die trying," Rolando replied.

A hush came over the court. A vow like this was not easily made, especially by one so young. The king, too, realized the gravity of Rolando's vow.

"Very well," the king said. "If you bring me one vial of water from the Fountain of Youth, I will give you my daughter in marriage and make you my heir." He turned to his daughter, and she stepped forward.

She smiled at Rolando and took his hand. "If you find the Fountain of Youth, I will marry you, and we will live forever," she said.

Rolando felt a shiver of love in his heart. What was happening was more than he had ever dared to dream.

"I will find it," he promised.

The king saw to it that Rolando received a horse and armor. He was given passage to the New World on a ship that would be sailing soon. All week, Rolando strutted around the court like a conquistador.

He walked with the king's daughter in the garden and again repeated his vow. "I will find the Fountain of Youth and bring back, not a vial of water, but a cask. Or I will die trying."

"You will not die, sir," the princess replied. "You will live forever." She kissed him, and Rolando's spirits soared.

How lucky I am, he thought, to have this opportunity.

My brothers slave in the orchards in the burning sun, and I am going to the New World. I will return with water from the Fountain of Youth and claim riches and the princess.

And so Rolando set sail for the Americas. Each day, he stood alone at the prow of the ship, dreaming of the adventure ahead of him.

"I will take the first drink from the Fountain of Youth, and I will never die," he said to himself. When he returned to his village with the princess at his side, the people would bow. His dream was worth any hardship that might lie ahead.

In Mexico City, Rolando immediately set out to search for someone to guide him north to the fabled lands of Calafia and her Amazons. Finally he found Temoc, an Aztec Indian who claimed he had visited the land of the Fountain of Youth.

Before the Spaniards conquered Mexico, the Aztecs used to send messengers and priests to trade in the lands they called Aztlán. Temoc had seen strange and magical sights. He had seen people who could run for days and nights and never tire. He had seen people turn into animals and travel through the jungle at night.

During the next few days, Rolando spent his time listening to Temoc's stories, and a bond of friendship grew between the two. Rolando was fascinated by Temoc's adventures, and the older man saw Rolando as the son he had never had.

"In that land of Cíbola, the cities are paved with gold," Temoc whispered in a hoarse voice. "I did not see the Fountain of Youth, but I talked to natives, who said it existed. But I warn you, do not go. There is much danger."

"I have sworn to my king to bring back a vial of water from the Fountain of Youth. Besides, if I drink from it, I cannot die. I will live forever and fear no danger."

"It is said an evil sorcerer guards the fountain," Temoc whispered. "He imprisons the souls of those who seek to drink from it."

"My sword will take care of the sorcerer," Rolando replied bravely. "Come with me and I will give you half of all the riches I find."

Temoc did not crave gold, but he admired Rolando's bravery. He also knew Rolando was determined but inexperienced. If he went north alone, he would surely die, but if Temoc helped him, he might stand a chance.

"I will go with you," he agreed. "But promise me that if I say we must turn back, we will."

"I promise," Rolando agreed.

With the gold coins the king of Spain had given him, Rolando bought supplies and a new saddle for his horse, Fuego. He also purchased burros to carry the supplies and for Temoc to ride. And an harquebus and gunpowder in case they met wild beasts or monsters.

When Rolando and Temoc were ready, they set out, leaving the grand Aztec capital behind them. For many weeks, they traveled north, crossing mountains and discovering native villages. At each village, Temoc spoke to the people in sign language, asking about the Fountain of Youth. And always the natives grew fearful when they understood the two men sought the fountain. They pointed north, saying there was a great river in that country.

"They say there is a río grande to the north," Temoc translated. "A river muy bravo. The people who live near the river can tell us how to find the fountain."

Rolando and Temoc crossed a wide desert and finally found the great river. They urged Fuego and the burros forward, hurrying to make camp before sunset.

That night, strange cries filled the dark. Temoc kept the campfire going, fearful of the creatures who haunted the river.

When there was no more wood for the fire and only embers illuminated the dark, a nebulous figure appeared. The burros fled in terror, carrying away all the supplies.

A voice spoke in the dark: "Turn back, foolish men. Do not seek immortality. Your quest will end in death!"

When the night creature had disappeared, a quaking Rolando turned to Temoc. "What was it?"

"A spirit of the river warning us not to go forward," Temoc said. "We must obey its command."

"Never," Rolando replied, breaking his promise to heed Temoc's warning. "I have only one goal, and that is to find the Fountain of Youth. For that, I will give anything I possess."

For the rest of the night, the two adventurers rested close to the dying fire. The noises of the spirit echoed in the dark, the haunting cry sounding like that of a grieving woman.

The next morning, Rolando and Temoc praised the sunlight for dissipating the night's vapors. They loaded Fuego with the few supplies they had left and continued their trek north.

In a few days, they came upon the plains of Cíbola. Here they were accosted by a band of Amazons, giant women who rode huge shaggy buffaloes. The Amazons came thundering down on Rolando and Temoc, overpowering and disarming the two explorers. Within moments, the frightened men's hands were securely tied.

"You are not welcome in our land," said the leader of the Amazons. "Tonight we will eat you and your horse for our dinner. The horse you ride does not compare to our steeds, the giant buffalo of the plains. He is skinny and worthless to us. Now you must gather firewood so we can cook our dinner."

The Amazons laughed and poked Rolando and Temoc; then they spent the afternoon playing games. They ran with huge boulders and tossed them to see who could throw them farthest. When the boulders hit the ground, they shook the earth and made a thunderous noise. The Amazons laughed and cheered, and they consumed great quantities of corn beer.

Nearby, under the watchful eye of a guard, Rolando and Temoc gathered and stacked firewood.

"I never thought I would gather the wood for my own roasting," Temoc moaned sadly.

"We're not cooked yet," Rolando muttered as they piled the wood. "Physically, we're no match for these Amazons, so we must use our wits. I have an idea. Let's slip our gunpowder pouches in with the logs. We'll see who gets roasted tonight."

The Amazon assigned to guard them did not see Rolando and Temoc slip their gunpowder pouches between the logs.

Dusk fell, and the giant women gathered, drunk and tired from their sport. They lit the fire, which was soon roaring. Then, as the Amazon cook turned toward Rolando and Temoc, there was a giant explosion that singed the eyelashes of the Amazons. They turned away in terror, unsure why the fire had exploded. In the confusion, Rolando and Temoc mounted Fuego, who had been tethered nearby, and escaped.

A few days later, they came to the land of the Two-Headed People, who lived along a tributary of the great river. The Two-Headed People feared those who had only one head, so they captured the two adventurers and tied them up.

Rolando and Temoc quickly realized that these people spent all their time arguing. One head would come up with an idea and the other would instantly disagree. All day and into the night, the two heads would argue, sometimes biting at each other in anger.

In spite of their constant quarreling, the Two-Headed People claimed to be twice as intelligent as anyone with only one head.

"If you're so smart," Rolando said, "tell me where I can find the Fountain of Youth."

"Searching for such a fantasy only proves how dumb you are," replied the leader of the Two-Headed People. "For possessing only one head, you are hereby sentenced to death."

"It's not fair to make me die because I have only one head," Rolando protested. He realized that to escape with his and Temoc's lives, he would have to be crafty. "There are some questions you can't answer," he said.

"We can answer *all* questions put to us!" the Two-Headed leader roared back.

Rolando remembered a question over which the lords and ladies of the court had spent long hours arguing.

"Very well," he said, "if you're so smart, tell us how many angels can sit on the head of a pin."

Each head had a different answer, and they started arguing and tearing at one another. During the fight, the two adventurers cut their bonds and ran away.

"By your wits, you're learning to survive in this mysterious land," Temoc said. "But you haven't met the greatest test. That will come when you meet the sorcerer who guards the Fountain of Youth. No one can outwit him. Let us turn back now."

"No," Rolando insisted. "I will find the fountain and drink of its water."

Rolando and Temoc pushed on, and finally they came to the land of many great pueblos. The people who lived in these adobe homes cultivated fields of corn, squash, and beans, living in harmony with the earth and their neighbors. They welcomed the adventurers.

These people are civilized, thought Rolando. Surely they know the secret location of the Fountain of Youth.

"Stay with us," a pueblo chief told Rolando. "You can settle here by the river, plant corn, and live in peace. I will give you one of my daughters as your wife."

"This is good advice," Temoc told his friend. "I am tired of traveling. Let us settle with these people."

"No," Rolando answered. "I cannot rest until I have found the fountain."

"Why do you seek eternal youth?" the elders of the pueblo asked him.

"I want to live forever," Rolando replied. "When I return home, I will have great wealth and the daughter of the king in marriage."

"Do not seek immortality," the elders counseled him. "It is unnatural. Every person, animal, and plant must die sometime. The day is born and dies; the seasons come and then pass away. That is the law of nature."

"I made a vow to be immortal!" Rolando cried. "And

my king and my wife will be immortal!"

Not heeding the chief's advice, he pushed on, and at each pueblo, he asked the same question: "Where is the Fountain of Youth?"

Finally, they found a very old man who answered them. "There," he whispered, and pointed to the mountain. "The ancients tell a story of a sorcerer, an evil magician who lives on the Mountain of Lost Souls. The evil man is a spirit who does not die. Do not go there."

"At last!" Rolando cried. "This is what I've sought!" He pushed his horse forward, commanding a reluctant Temoc to follow, urging them up the high mountain and into the forest.

On the mountain peak, the wind moaned like a restless spirit. The forest was dark and menacing. No birds sang in the trees, and no deer ran on the trails. All was silent and eerie. In the middle of the forest stood a dark castle built of stone.

"This is the Castle of Lost Souls," Temoc said. "It is a prison for those who have searched for false goals. Let us turn away before we are captured."

"No! We are near the Fountain of Youth!" Rolando exclaimed. "I'm sure this is it!"

As they approached the castle, the sorcerer appeared. He was dressed in a splendid gold suit like the genies of long ago. Rubies, diamonds, and precious emeralds glittered on his fingers and in necklaces around his throat. He cracked a whip whose sound rolled like thunder down the mountain.

He greeted Rolando with a pleasant smile. "Welcome to my castle, great adventurer."

"Let's turn back while we have a chance," the frightened Temoc said.

"This is the magician who guards the Fountain of Youth," Rolando said. "He doesn't look too fearful."

"But no one has ever returned from here," Temoc whispered, looking at the dark prison. From within its walls came the mournful cries of lost souls.

"Welcome, oh great adventurer," the sorcerer repeated. "What is it you seek?"

"I have come seeking the Fountain of Youth," Rolando answered.

"Many have sought the fountain before you," the magician replied, "but to drink of the waters of immortality, you must give me something in return."

"What would you barter for?" asked Rolando.

"The price is high," the sorcerer said.

"Name it and it shall be yours," said the confident Rolando. He had not come this far to be turned away.

"You may drink from the fountain if you sell me your soul."

Temoc gasped. "Do not do it." He knew that once a

man sold his soul, he could never rest in peace.

Even Rolando hesitated. He had not expected the price to be so high. "Can I trust you?" he asked.

"Of course you can trust me," the sorcerer replied. "If I fail to keep my promise, then you not only get a drink from the fountain but I will be your slave forever. I can deliver anything you desire."

"Will you keep your word?" Rolando asked.

"A magician never lies," the sorcerer replied.

"Then you will make me immortal?"

"As I promise," the sorcerer answered. "You will live forever."

In the Prison of Lost Souls, the imprisoned spirits cried in agony. Even Rolando trembled when he heard their plaintive cries.

"Who are they?" he asked.

"Bad losers," the sorcerer replied, and cracked his whip to quiet them down.

"Don't believe the sorcerer!" Temoc cried, but it was too late. Rolando was ready to make his bargain with the sorcerer.

"Give me a drink from the fountain and you may have my soul," he said.

They went to the courtyard of the castle, where a gushing fountain was surrounded by a tangled mass of green plants. The trees and bushes swayed back and forth.

The sorcerer offered Rolando a cupful of water from the fountain. As he drank, he felt a numbness; then a sleep like death overcame him and he dropped to the ground. The evil magician pulled Rolando's soul from his body.

"You see!" The evil magician laughed. "Your soul will live forever, but in my prison! The immortality I promised is yours!"

Rolando's soul cried as he realized he had been deceived. Yes, he would live forever, but it would be in the Prison of Lost Souls. He would spend eternity with the other zealous adventurers who, like him, had come looking for the fountain. They had all made a deal with the sorcerer, and they had lost.

Before his soul disappeared into the dark dungeons of the prison, Rolando turned to Temoc. "Go and warn all those who seek their fortune never to sell their souls to evil!"

With that, he disappeared into the prison.

A frightened Temoc mounted Fuego and rode down the mountain. For weeks, he urged the exhausted horse south, following the route back to Mexico City.

Later, in the mercados of the great city, Temoc told the tragic story of his friend to anyone who would listen. Some sympathetic listeners shook their heads and tossed a few coins in his cup. They thought the old Indian was crazy, or merely telling a wild fantasy for coins to buy his next meal.

A few young men listened attentively and began to

dream of immortality. Some asked the old man if he knew the way north to the Fountain of Youth.

"I have told you this story so you will not dream of immortality," Temoc replied.

But the young men did not listen. They began to dream of the Fountain of Youth and began to make plans to travel north in search of it.

The Lost Camel

In the village of La Mesilla, near Las Cruces, there lived a poor widow and her son. She made her living by washing clothes for the family of the rich landowner, and her son, Adán, helped her.

The widow washed the clothes in a large tub, and when they were rinsed, Adán hung them out to dry. In this way, mother and son made enough money to support themselves.

The summer Adán turned thirteen, he grew restless. He felt he was grown-up enough to go out into the world and earn a living. Sometimes the neighboring boys made fun of him because his mother was a washerwoman.

One day, Adán said to his mother, "It is time

121

for me to go and look for work. You work very hard and long hours. I must begin to help support you."

"What kind of work would you find, my son? You are too young. The landowner won't hire you to hoe or pick chile in the fields. Only grown men are hired."

"I was at the post office yesterday," Adán replied, "and I heard the men talking about a lost camel. There was a picture of the animal posted on the wall."

"A camel in New Mexico?" Adán's mother was surprised. She had heard of a lot of strange things in her beloved land, but never a camel.

"Yes. Since the War between the States ended, a United States Army unit stationed at Fort Selden is experimenting with camels to carry loads across the desert to California."

"But what does this have to do with you?" she asked.

"The army is offering a reward for the lost camel. If I find it, we will have enough money to live on for a long time."

Adán's mother protested. She felt her son was too young to go out into the world to earn a living. Besides, looking for such a strange animal beyond the confines of the safe village seemed dangerous to her. More and more cowboys from Texas were appearing in the village. They brought their cattle to sell to the army, and she was afraid they might kidnap her son. But Adán persisted, and finally she relented.

"Very well," she said. "But take this medal of the Virgin Mary with you. Pray to her every day for guidance."

"I will," Adán promised.

She packed a gunnysack with provisions, which Adán loaded on his burro.

He knelt in front of his mother and she gave him her blessing. "May God and the Virgin watch over you. Say your prayers every night."

"I will, Mamá. Adiós."

"Adiós," she replied, tears welling in her eyes.

"Don't be sad. You'll see, I'll return with money to take care of you."

Adán headed north toward Socorro, where he had heard the camel had been lost.

He traveled five miles that first day, following the Río Grande. At times, he paused to let his burro drink at the river, and to rest under the huge cottonwood trees.

That evening, he made camp and hobbled the burro so it would not stray during the night. He started a campfire, warmed the meat and tortillas his mother had given him, and ate. Then, exhausted from the day's journey, he curled up in his bedroll.

Above him, the Milky Way glittered like a necklace of diamonds. Coyotes howled in the hills, and somewhere in the river bosque he heard the scream of a cougar. Adán trembled. He was many miles from home, alone.

He closed his eyes. Tightly holding the medal his mother had given him, he began to say his prayers.

"Dear Virgin Mary, please keep me safe. Don't let the wild animals eat me or my burro. I need to find the lost camel so my mother does not have to work so hard."

He heard something rustle, and he opened his eyes. A woman dressed in a blue robe stood by the dying fire. She wore a crown of gold, and angels seemed to hover around her. Adán sat up.

"Who are you?" he asked in a tremulous voice.

"I am the Virgin Mary," the beautiful woman replied.

"Am I dreaming?" asked Adán.

"No, you are not dreaming," the Virgin replied. "I travel the roads and watch over people. What are you doing so far from home?"

"I'm looking for a lost camel," Adán replied. "If I find it, I will get a reward and help support my mother."

"But how will you find the camel in this wilderness? The river stretches far to the north, and on either side is the desert. There are few settlements in this area."

"That is true," said Adán. "I know nothing about camels. But I do want to help my mother."

"To find the camel, you will need to learn how to track it."

"Perhaps I will meet someone on the road who can teach me to follow its tracks," replied an undaunted Adán.

"Yes, there are honest men along this road who could teach you the skills you need," replied the Virgin. "But there are also dishonest men who will offer to teach you. They are thieves who will only want to steal your burro."

"How will I know who is honest and who is dishonest?"

"Take these three apples," the Virgin Mary said. "If someone offers to help you, cut an apple in two parts, and make one side smaller than the other. Offer to share the apple. If the man takes the bigger part, then he is a thief. But the man who takes the smaller part will be a friend you can trust."

Adán thanked the Virgin and tucked the apples into his pocket. He slept well that night, and early the next morning he was on his way.

That evening, as he was having his supper of cold tortillas and meat, a man appeared. He was a bearded fur trapper who was looking for beaver along the river. Adán invited the man to share his meal, and as they ate, Adán told him about his search for the lost camel.

"I can teach you to track any animal," the man bragged. "Let us travel together. When we find the camel, we will return it to the army and share the reward."

Adán wasn't sure this foul-smelling man was to be trusted. Then he remembered the Virgin's advice. He took one of the apples and cut it in two. He offered the pieces to the trapper, who took the bigger part and ate it greedily.

Night fell, and Adán only pretended to go to sleep. When he heard the fur trapper snoring like a bear, he got up, quietly gathered his sack of provisions, and hurried to his burro. He walked all night until he was sure he was safely away from the trapper.

A day later, Adán met another man on the road. This

man made his living hunting mountain lions, which raided herds of sheep and killed the lambs. He was a big man, loud and boisterous. His fur cap was made from a mountain lion's head.

"That's a nice burro you have there," the man said. "I could use a burro like that on my hunts. Horses are afraid of the smell of mountain lions, but a burro is not."

Adán was suspicious of the man, but nevertheless he invited him to share his meal. The hunter wolfed down the meat and tortillas Adán offered him, keeping his own provisions to himself. When they were finished eating, Adán told him of his quest for the lost camel.

"I am the best hunter in New Mexico," the man boasted. "Let us travel together. I will teach you how to track the lost camel. If we find it, we can share the reward."

Adán took the second apple from his pocket and cut it in two. He offered the pieces to the man, and the hunter grabbed the bigger part. In a few crunches, it was down his throat.

"I have never tasted such a sweet apple," he said, greedily eyeing Adán's part.

Night fell and the hunter wrapped himself in his furs and was soon snoring. Adán quietly gathered his provisions and hurried to his burro.

"We must leave quietly," he whispered to the burro. "This man is not to be trusted."

Adán continued north, following the river, looking for

signs of the lost camel. He grew frustrated, for although he had seen a picture of the camel the army had posted on the post office wall, he didn't know what kind of tracks a camel made.

Late the next day, Adán met a vaquero. The cowboy was a handsome man, about the age of Adán's mother, and he handled his horse like an expert.

The vaquero greeted Adán, "Buenos días, muchacho."

"Buenos días, señor."

"Are you lost?"

"No, señor," replied Adán. "I am hunting."

"It's a hot day to hunt," said the vaquero. He got down from his horse and shared his water with Adán. As they sat under the shade of a cottonwood tree, the vaquero told Adán his plans for the future.

"I am going to Mexico to seek my fortune. The rich landowners pay good money to their vaqueros. I will save my money, and when I return, I will have enough to buy land and have my own ranchito."

Adán liked the man. He reminded him vaguely of his father, whom he had known only as a young child. But he grew suspicious when the vaquero admired his burro.

"I only ride horses," the vaquero said, "but for carrying provisions on a dangerous trail, nothing can beat the humble burro."

They talked and Adán told the vaquero about the lost camel.

"If I find the camel, I can claim the reward. With the money, I can help support my mother."

"You are a good son," the vaquero said. "Maybe I can help you. I know how to track cattle that wander away from the herd into the desert. I think the camel's tracks are much like a cow's, maybe bigger. But when you track an animal, there are all kinds of signs you watch for. A broken twig or fur caught on a mesquite bush can lead you to the animal even when there are no tracks."

"Very well," Adán agreed. "I need to learn all these things. Will you share my meal?"

"Gladly," the vaquero replied. "You start a fire and I will hunt for a rabbit."

By the time Adán had a roaring fire going, the vaquero returned with a rabbit, which he put on a spit to roast. They ate, and when they were done, Adán took out the last apple the Virgin Mary had given him. He cut it in two parts and offered them to the vaquero. The cowboy politely took the smaller piece.

This is a good companion who can teach me what I need to know, Adán thought. That night, he slept soundly, confident that the vaquero meant him no harm.

When he awoke, the vaquero was gone. Adán leapt up and looked for his burro, but it, too, was nowhere in sight.

"Oh, I shouldn't have trusted that man!" he cried. He raced around the camp, shouting for help.

"Over here," he heard the vaquero call. Adán ran to the

river and found the vaquero watering his horse and Adán's burro.

"Our steeds need to drink for the day ahead," the vaquero said. "As soon as we have breakfast, we will start looking for the lost camel."

Adán let out a sigh of relief. Here truly was a companion he could trust. They searched all day. The vaquero taught Adán how to read the signs of animals who had used the river trails.

"See here? A herd of cattle was being driven from Mexico to Alburquerque."

"How do you know they are Mexican cattle?" Adán asked.

"The cattle here weigh less, so they leave a fainter print on the ground. And this is the time of year the Mexican vaqueros bring their cattle north to sell."

Adán nodded, pleased to have learned this.

"Here a bear and her cub dug for roots," the vaquero said, and he explained the signs to Adán.

For days, they traveled up and down the trail, and Adán learned many of a tracker's skills.

Finally, they found the camel's tracks by the river.

"Tracks like these, I have never seen before," said the vaquero. "They must belong to the camel. He has been hiding up in the hills, but I knew sooner or later he would have to come down for a drink of water. He's been lost two weeks and he is thirsty."

"Yes," Adán replied, "and it looks like he is still carrying the bags of provisions. The bag on his left side is loaded with wheat."

The vaquero was surprised. "How do you know that?"

"The bag must have been ripped by a branch," said Adán. "See here where the grains of wheat have dropped on the ground?"

"You're right," the vaquero said, laughing. "Looks like I have trained an excellent tracker."

"And on his right side, he was carrying a large jug of honey."

Again the vaquero was surprised. "How do you know?"

"The jug is leaking. See here where the ants have gathered to swarm and eat the honey."

"¡Muy bien!" the vaquero exclaimed. "Your sharp eyes see even more signs than mine."

"The camel is blind in one eye," Adán continued as he read the signs near the camel tracks, "and he has one tooth missing."

The vaquero shook his head. "I won't believe that until we catch the camel."

They followed the tracks down to the river and found the camel near the water. The vaquero quickly and expertly lassoed it. The big animal grew calm when Adán came close with his burro.

"The sack of wheat and the jug of honey are still tied to its back," said Adán.

"Yes, but let's see if he's blind and missing one tooth," his friend replied.

They checked the camel, and sure enough, he was blind in one eye. When the vaquero pulled up the camel's lip, he found one tooth missing.

"How did you know?" the puzzled man asked Adán.

"I read the signs carefully, as you taught me. I noticed he grazed only on one side of the path. That told me he was blind. Where he chomped at grass, he left a slight clump in the middle of the bite."

"You have become an expert tracker, amigo, and you deserve the reward," the vaquero cried.

"We will share it equally," Adán replied, "for you have taught me many valuable lessons."

They led the camel back to the army fort near Las Cruces and were given the reward. Adán divided the silver coins equally and insisted the vaquero take his fair share.

Then they rode to La Mesilla, where Adán's mother was overjoyed to see her son return home safely.

"My son! My son!" she cried. "Gracias a Dios. You are home safe."

When Adán showed her his reward, she nearly fainted.

"But where did you get so much money?" she asked, looking from Adán to the vaquero, who stood nearby.

Adán introduced his friend and told his mother the story. When he was done, his mother invited the vaquero to stay for supper. She prepared a big meal, and as they ate,

Adán and the vaquero again told the story of tracking the lost camel.

The vaquero did not continue on to Mexico to work on a big hacienda. Instead, he bought a small ranch nearby with his share of the reward. He invited Adán to work with him and partake equally in the profits.

Every evening after work, they rode from the fields to eat with Adán's mother. Soon the vaquero began to court Adán's mother, and shortly thereafter, they were married.

With training from his stepfather, Adán became one of the most expert vaqueros in the region. Their ranch prospered. And whenever a person or an animal was lost, the neighbors immediately came to Adán for help.

The Miller's Good Luck

One evening as they were having dinner at El Farol, a restaurant in Las Cruces, two rich merchants got into an argument. The waitress paid no attention, for the men were well-known customers of the restaurant, and everyone knew they were old friends who loved to argue.

That night, the two men were arguing about the role of luck in a person's life. Was it luck or careful planning that made the man?

"Luck plays the most important role in a man's life," Libor said. "Look at me. I made my fortune by pure luck. I won three hundred dollars in a card game. I bought a store, and now I'm the richest merchant in all Doña Ana County."

"No, no!" his friend Vidal answered. "It's not luck that makes the man. One has to work hard and invest for the future. Then one's fortune grows little by little. I made my fortune because I invested my money. I was a poor chile vendor, but each month I put away a little in savings. With time, I was able to buy the fields I own. Now I am the richest farmer in the valley."

"No, it's luck," insisted Libor.

Their voices rose as they argued.

"Work hard and plan ahead!" exclaimed Vidal.

"Fate brings one good luck or misfortune!" countered Libor.

"Let's put our theories to a test," Vidal said in exasperation.

"How?"

"First, let us find a poor but honorable man. We will give him a sum of money to do with as he pleases. Later, we'll check on him and see what he has done with it. That way, we can judge whether the luck of receiving the money makes him prosper, or if he remains as he was before."

"Excellent idea," agreed Libor.

They parted in good spirits and forgot about their argument. It so happened that a month later they had to travel together to Santa Fe on business. They filled their carts with goods and started up the Camino Real, passing Socorro and Alburquerque on the way. Near Bernalillo, one of the carts broke down, so they stopped at the blacksmith's shop to have it repaired. While they were waiting, they noticed a small mill near the river.

"Who owns that mill?" Libor asked the smithy.

"Pedro Bernal," the smithy answered. "A hardworking man."

"Is he honest?"

"He is honest, but very poor. He hardly makes enough to feed his family."

The two friends looked at each other.

"Remember our conversation about the role of luck in a man's life?" asked Libor.

"Yes, I do. We still haven't settled the argument."

"So, why don't we test our idea on the miller?"

"I agree," replied Vidal, and together they walked to the miller's shop. "Good friend," Vidal called to the miller. "Are you an honest man?"

"Yes, I am," replied Pedro Bernal. "I grind wheat and corn for the farmers, and I have never taken advantage of a customer. I value my reputation above all things."

"My friend and I would like to put you to a test," said Vidal. "Allow us to give you one hundred pesos. You may do anything you wish with the money."

"Why would you give me a hundred pesos?" asked Pedro, nervous at the very idea. Most farmers from the area paid him with wheat, corn, apples, or vegetables. Some paid with beef or poultry. Few paid him with coins. He had never seen that much money in his life.

"It's just a bet my friend and I have. We mean no ill will toward you. The money is yours to use any way you want."

Pedro looked at the shiny coins. He needed a burro for the mill, a new roof for his home, and many other things. If he took the money, he could make these improvements. But he had always been an independent man, and he believed only in what he earned. He knew of a man from Sandia who had found a fortune, but the wealth had made his life miserable.

"All right," he said, after considering his answer carefully. "I'll take the money."

His hands shook as he received the coins. This is my lucky day, he thought. I didn't earn this, and here it is!

The two merchants said good-bye and went on their way to Santa Fe.

Pedro put the coins in a leather bag and spent the rest of the afternoon wondering what to do with the money.

The first thing I should do is buy food for my family, he thought as he closed his shop. He went to the village store and bought a leg of lamb.

On the way home, he stopped to rest. He placed the meat and the bag of pesos beside him. As Pedro was nodding off, a large hawk circling overhead saw the leg of lamb and dove for it. Just as the hawk was about to clutch the lamb in its talons, Pedro jumped up and grabbed the meat. The hawk swerved, seized the bag with the pesos, and flew off with it.

"Oh, poor me," groaned Pedro, "to save the meat, I lost

the money. I have no luck. Now I am the same poor miller I have always been."

When he arrived home, his wife, Mela, and his many children greeted him at the door. "Why so sad, dear husband?" his wife asked.

Pedro told his family what had happened.

"Have faith," his wife said when he was done. "Maybe someday our luck will change. In the meantime, I'm going to cook the meat for dinner."

A week later, Libor and Vidal were on their way back to Las Cruces. They had sold their goods, and with the profit, they had bought beautiful Chimayó rugs. When they sold these rugs in Las Cruces, they would triple their money.

When they came to Bernalillo, they stopped by the miller's place.

"What has transpired in your life since we gave you the hundred pesos?" Libor asked.

"Did you put it in the bank or invest in land as any wise man would do?" asked Vidal.

Pedro hung his head. He was afraid they would think the story of the hawk was a lie, but he told them anyway. He was so persuasive that Libor and Vidal believed him.

"Let's try again," said Vidal.

"I agree." Libor nodded.

"No," pleaded Pedro, "find someone else to give the money to."

"No, no," the two insisted. "You are an honest man. Take

these hundred pesos. You may do whatever you desire with the money."

So Pedro took the money and the two men drove away, promising to see him in a few months.

I don't want to make a mistake this time, thought Pedro. I won't stop anywhere until I get home. He wrapped the coins in a bundle and ran home to tell his wife. She wasn't there when he arrived, so he looked around for a place to hide the money. He found a clay jar filled with wheat in the pantry.

"This wheat has been here a year and no one has used it," he said. "It's a perfect place to hide the money."

He emptied the wheat on the table, placed the bundle at the bottom of the jar, then covered it with the grains.

"There! It's safe!" Pleased with himself, Pedro went back to work.

Late that afternoon when he returned home, his wife greeted him at the door with a smile.

"You look happy, viejo," she said.

"I am very happy," he replied. "But you are, too. Did you kill our only hen to make soup?"

"No. I made an excellent deal today," she replied. "Look." She showed him a new tablecloth on the table. "Isn't it pretty? I haven't had a new cloth in ages."

"Very nice," Pedro said. "But where did you get the money to buy such an elegant tablecloth?"

"Money? You know we have no money. I traded for it."

"What did you trade?"

"You remember that old jar of wheat we had in the pantry? A traveling salesman took it for the tablecloth."

"Oh no," Pedro groaned. He rushed to the pantry. Sure enough, his wife had traded the jar in which he had hidden the money.

"Who was the man?" Pedro shouted.

"I've never seen him before," replied his surprised wife. "He said he lives near Placitas, but I don't know him."

Pedro slumped into a chair. "We're cursed, we're cursed," he cried.

"What are you talking about?"

Pedro told her the story. "You have traded a fortune for a tablecloth that costs a few pesos," he moaned.

"Have faith," his wife said, trying to console him. "Perhaps it's not our fate to have fortune or good luck."

So Pedro was consoled and went back to his work as usual. Months later, the two merchants from Las Cruces came up the dusty road again, their burros loaded with goods to sell in Santa Fe. They stopped to visit with Pedro, and he told them the entire story.

"I find this hard to believe," Vidal complained to his partner. "Twice he has told us wild stories."

"It's only that luck has been against him," said Libor. "Look around you. He is as poor as he was when we first met him."

"Let's be on our way," Vidal insisted. "I'll squander no more money on this poor fellow."

"Very well," Libor agreed, turning to Pedro. "Oh, by the way, here's a worthless piece of lead I've been carrying. May it bring you good luck." He laughed, and the two drove away.

"At least no one will steal this worthless piece of lead," Pedro said. That afternoon he took it home with him.

While Pedro and his family were eating supper, his neighbor came by.

"Buenas tardes, vecino. I'm going fishing tomorrow, but I have no lead for my lines. Do you have any you can spare?"

Pedro offered him the lead the merchant had given him and wished his neighbor good luck.

"Thank you," the man said. "I promise you that the first fish I catch is yours."

"Think nothing of it," Pedro replied. The next day, he went to work as usual, and when he returned home that afternoon, he found his wife cooking a big fish.

"Where did you get the fish?" asked Pedro.

"Our neighbor brought it to us. Don't you remember? He promised to give us the first fish he caught."

Pedro grunted. He was hungry and the frying fish smelled wonderful. That's all that mattered.

"Well, you wouldn't believe what I found in the stomach of the fish when I cleaned it," his wife continued.

"What?"

"A beautiful piece of glass." She showed him the large piece of glass, which glittered brightly.

"It is beautiful, but worthless," said Pedro, tossing it aside.

"Take it to the jeweler and see if he can make a necklace from it," his wife suggested. "Maybe he'll give you a few pesos for it."

The next day, Pedro put the glass in his pocket, and on his way to work, he stopped at the jeweler's shop.

The jeweler greeted Pedro. "Buenos días. How can I help you today?"

Pedro took out the piece of glass and showed it to the jeweler. "How much will you give me for this?"

The jeweler examined the object and nearly choked. It was a priceless diamond. He had never seen anything as valuable in the village of Bernalillo. In Santa Fe, he could sell it for a fortune.

"Ah," he stammered. "It's pretty glass, but almost worthless. I'll give you five pesos."

Pedro was about to say yes when a fly landed on his nose. "¡Oyé!" he said loudly, swiping at it. The jeweler took Pedro's exclamation to mean no.

"Okay, okay, I'll give you a hundred pesos!" he exclaimed, eager to have the beautiful diamond.

Pedro was flabbergasted. Why would the jeweler suddenly increase his price? Ah well, a hundred pesos for a piece of glass was great. He was about to say yes when the same fly landed on his ear.

"Shh!" Pedro exclaimed, and threw up his arms.

The jeweler shrank back. Obviously, Pedro knew the value of the diamond and was very irritated at such a low price.

"Very well!" he cried. "I'll give you fifty thousand pesos for the diamond!"

Pedro's mouth dropped. Fifty thousand pesos? A diamond? It seemed impossible. Was the jeweler pulling his leg?

"You joke with me," stammered Pedro.

"No, my friend," said the worried jeweler, thinking he had insulted Pedro. He tried to soothe him. "I would not dream of joking with you. I'll give you seventy-five thousand pesos. That's my last offer."

"Bueno," Pedro replied, quaking in his boots. "I'll take it."

"You drive a tough bargain," the jeweler said, going to his safe for the money. "I have bargained all my life, and I've never met anyone as good as you."

Pedro held the bundle of money in his trembling hands. No one in the village had this much money. He hurried home to tell his wife what had happened.

His wife was equally surprised. "What are you going to do with so much money?" she asked.

"I'll invest it in the mill. Make it larger so I can serve more farmers. And we always wanted a summer cottage at the foot of the Sandia Mountains. Now we can build one. What's left, we can put in the bank for our old age."

With much excitement, Pedro and his wife set out to do all these things. In a few months, the mill was prospering beyond their dreams. They built their cottage and took the family there on weekends. The money they saved in the bank earned them interest, and they grew very prosperous.

A year passed, and one day while Pedro was sitting in his office at the mill, the two merchants from Las Cruces drove up with their carts full of Santo Domingo jewelry they were taking home to sell. Pedro rushed out to greet them.

"My, my," one of the merchants said. "We see you have expanded your mill."

The two men admired the new building, the busy workers, the goodwill that seemed part of the enterprise. Pedro was now an employer who hired many men to work for him.

"You have made many improvements," Vidal said. "How did all this come about?"

Pedro told them the story of the diamond his wife had found in the fish and how he had sold it.

"So it was pure luck that made you wealthy!" Libor exclaimed.

"Wait a minute!" interjected Vidal. "I just don't believe his story."

The merchant's lack of confidence made Pedro sad.

"I wish there were some way I could prove what has happened," he said. "But since that's impossible, please stay and have lunch. After we eat, I want to show you my cabin at the foot of the mountain."

The two merchants agreed, and after a wonderful feast, Pedro's servants saddled three of his finest horses. Then the three men, followed by Pedro's servants, rode up the mountain. The merchants admired the cabin. Here was a man who only a year ago had been a poor miller. Now he had the home of a rich man, a thriving business, a wonderful mountain house, many servants, whom he paid well, and money in the bank. How did all this happen?

Later in the afternoon, when they stopped at a stream to enjoy a cool drink, they spied a huge nest on the branch of a tall pine tree.

"What is that?" asked Vidal.

"A hawk's nest," replied Pedro.

"I've never seen one. Let's have a closer look at it."

Pedro ordered one of his servants to climb the tree and bring the nest down for inspection. When the hawk's nest was on the ground, they examined it carefully. The servant noticed a tattered bag at the bottom of the nest and pulled it out.

Pedro instantly recognized the leather bag. "That's the bag the hawk stole from me!" he cried.

"The bag with the first hundred pesos we gave you?" asked Libor.

"The same!"

"Then the money should be in it."

Pedro eagerly tore at the weathered bag, and, sure enough, out fell the coins.

"You told us the truth," Vidal said. "You are an honest man."

They congratulated the miller and slapped him on the back.

They rode down to Placitas and stopped to rest their horses. Since they had not brought wheat or bran for the horses to eat, Pedro sent one of his servants to buy grain at the home of a man who used to be a traveling salesman. The servant quickly returned with a clay jar of wheat.

"It's old wheat," said the servant, "but it's been well covered. The horses will eat it."

When he emptied the clay jar to feed the horses, out dropped a bundle.

Pedro, who immediately recognized the jar, took the bundle. "This is the same clay jar in which I hid the second hundred pesos you gave me," he told the merchants.

"Let's have a look at it," said Libor. He tore the rags open and out fell the money. "You told us the truth about this incident, too, for here is the money," he said.

They praised Pedro. He was truly an honest man. Now they believed his story of the diamond his wife had found in the fish. But they still couldn't decide if it was luck or planning ahead that had made the miller a wealthy man.

✑ Sipa's Choice

Long ago in the pine forests of the northern Rocky Mountains, a man climbed a mountain peak to pray. This was Flint Man, the leader of a tribe of people who were camped in the valley below. The sun had not yet risen when Flint Man left his tepee to climb the mountain.

From this peak, Flint Man prayed daily to the Sun God. As the sun rose, Flint Man raised his arms in thanksgiving. He prayed that he might be wise and able to lead his people to lands where there would be food and safety. He especially prayed that his son's health be restored.

The son of Flint Man, Sipa, had been only thirteen when he was attacked by a grizzly bear during a hunting trip. He had found bear tracks, and instead of telling his father, he followed the tracks

149

alone. Around a bend in the forest trail, he came upon a giant grizzly. Sensing his territory had been invaded, the bear attacked.

Luckily, Flint Man and the other warriors were nearby. They heard Sipa's cries and came swiftly. Their arrows killed the bear, but the damage was already done. Sipa's left leg was badly mauled.

The medicine man set the leg, but it didn't heal properly. Sipa needed a stick to support himself when he walked. The entire village knew that a boy with a crippled leg could never be a warrior or a chief. Flint Man grew very sad, and daily he went up the mountain alone to pray for guidance.

One morning the Sun God answered his prayers, sending a golden eagle to land on a nearby tree. Through the eagle, the Sun God spoke to Flint Man.

"Take your people far to the south. There, where the great Rocky Mountains end, lies the River of the Sun. Bathe your son in the river and he will regain his ability to walk."

A very grateful Flint Man hurried back to his village to tell his people what the eagle had told him. All grew excited as they took down their tepees and made preparations to move.

"The journey will be very difficult for you," Flint Man told his son.

"We must go, Father," Sipa said. "I did not follow the instructions you gave me for the hunt, and the bear taught me a lesson. Now I have a second chance."

So they wandered south, along the spine of the mountains, in search of the River of the Sun. They suffered many hardships during their journey, but they never forgot to thank the Sun God. Every day, the families rose to greet the sun and say a prayer of thanks. They offered cornmeal to the sun, scattering it to the east, in the direction of the sunrise.

The Sun God looked on Flint Man and his people with favor. The golden eagle appeared daily to lead them through the perilous mountains.

The journey was long and arduous. Often the hunters went out but returned empty-handed. The women had only the dried jerky from the prior season's hunting to cook in the evenings. Some of the people grew discouraged and forgot to pray to the Sun God. But not Flint Man. In the morning, he rose to offer prayers; then, without eating breakfast, he strapped his son to a travois and pulled it throughout the day.

For weeks, they traveled south. Flint Man grew gaunt and tired, but he never complained. He dreamed of the river water that would cure his son.

One day, the golden eagle landed and perched on top of a towering pine tree.

"Look, Father," Sipa said, "this is surely a sign we are close to the River of the Sun."

"It is true," Flint Man replied. "My prayers have been answered. But I am growing old, and the journey has been difficult. Soon you must lead the tribe."

Sipa grew sad. How could he be a great leader like his father when he could walk only with the help of a stick?

At that moment, the scouts, who had gone ahead, came back over the ridge and signaled they had found the River of the Sun. A great cry went up from the people as they rushed forward.

What they saw made them utter prayers of thanksgiving. Red cliffs protected the valley. On the mesas above the valley grew piñon and juniper trees. In the canyon below, a clear river ran, reflecting the bright blue sky. The valley was lush and green with grass for the horses. There were many deer, turkey, and other game. There was enough land to plant corn and squash.

Flint Man raised his arms in thanks. Once again, the Sun God spoke to him in the form of the eagle.

"This is the River of the Sun," the Sun God said. "In this valley, you may build your homes and plant your crops. Here you can plant fields of maize, beans, and squash. The water of the river is sweet to drink."

Then the Sun God directed the people to the riverbank. Large golden fish swam in the water.

"These are the golden carp," said the Sun God. "They are my sacred fish. You must never eat them."

"We will never disturb the golden carp," Flint Man told the Sun God. "They will be like brothers and sisters to us. My son, Sipa, who will one day be leader of my people, will care for the fish."

"That is a promise you must honor if your people are to survive," the Sun God said. Then the golden eagle lifted its great wings and flew away, disappearing into the sunlight.

Flint Man lifted his son in his arms and waded into the cold, bubbling river. He dipped his son in the water and chanted a prayer.

Sipa felt the chill of the water. His mangled left leg throbbed and he felt like drawing it out of the water. Then he felt energy coursing through both his legs, and with the help of his father, he stood. He felt his leg grow strong beneath him.

"I feel my strength returning," he whispered.

"The Sun God has kept his promise. You are healed," said Flint Man.

Sipa took a few steps forward. On the bank, the people waited expectantly. Those who had doubted Flint Man now realized his vision had been real. They saw Sipa take his first steps without the aid of a stick and knew the healing was a miracle. Soon he would be strong enough to join the hunters who went to bring meat to the people.

A joyous cheer went up as Sipa walked by himself to the bank. Now everyone knew the Sun God watched over them, and they felt renewed.

The men got busy and cleared the land, and the women planted corn, squash, beans, and chile. Together, they built homes of mud bricks and stone. By midsummer, the people were eating fresh vegetables, and everyone's health improved. In the fall, they gathered their harvest.

"We must have a fiesta to thank the Sun God," Flint Man told his people. He was an old man now. His hair was gray and he hobbled slowly when he walked. The people respected him because he had brought them to a land of plenty.

All morning, the women roasted ears of fresh green corn and pumpkins. They cooked pots of beans flavored with chile. They made bread from ground corn. The aroma of cooking food spread throughout the village, and everybody was happy.

Before they ate, Flint Man, his son, and the elders took the bread to the river to feed the golden fish. They dropped pieces of the bread into the water and thanked the Sun God. In the Valley of the Sun, all were happy and at peace.

That winter, Flint Man fell very ill. His family gathered around him in the warmth of his home.

"I am happy to have seen the valley," he told his family. "Now Sipa will be your chief. Do not forget to honor the Sun God," he said to his son.

"I will not forget my duties, Father," Sipa replied.

Flint Man died and was buried with great ceremony. For some time, Sipa continued the ceremonies. But after a while, Sipa forgot to feed the golden fish. He spent his days gambling and hunting with the other young men.

That winter, terrible blizzards came down from the north. The people had saved corn and jerky, but the provisions began to run out. The hunters went looking for game, but the snow was so high, they returned empty-handed.

Sipa sent the priests to pray to the Sun God, but the storms did not abate. Storm after storm swept over the land, and the people huddled in their cold homes.

Sipa grew angry with the Sun God.

"Why doesn't the Sun God answer my prayers?" he asked the elders.

"You have not fed the golden fish of the river," the elders said.

"Bah! Those ceremonies mean nothing!" Sipa retorted. "I depend only on myself."

He sent the warriors out into the snow to find game. They broke through the thick snowdrifts until their feet froze, but they found no deer. All winter, the people battled hunger.

That spring, the people hurried to plant their gardens. The corn sprouted, but not a drop of rain fell. Soon the crops withered and died. Green meadows turned dry and brown. The sun scorched the land, burning everything in sight. There was no food to be found, and the people again went hungry.

The River of the Sun dried to a trickle, but the golden carp swam in the few deep pools that remained.

Sipa's people came to him. "There is no food to eat. Our children are dying of hunger. You must do something."

"Pray to the Sun God," the elders advised.

"I cannot depend on the Sun God," Sipa replied. "He has not answered our prayers. First the cold winter and now there is no rain. I will take the hunters to find game."

They went far in all directions, but they found no game. The old people began to die of hunger.

Again Sipa's people came to him.

"I cannot bear to see my children hungry," a man said. "We must eat the golden fish to stay alive."

"We cannot," the elders replied. "Flint Man promised the Sun God never to eat his fish."

"What do you say, Sipa?" the people asked.

Sipa thought a long time. Yes, he had promised his father never to harm the golden fish, but he felt the Sun God had turned away from him. If they didn't eat the golden fish, they would starve. If they ate the fish, he would break his vow.

Sipa finally spoke. "Our hunters have gone far in all directions, and they have found no game. The fields are dry. There is no corn left in our pit houses. If we are to survive, we must eat the golden fish."

He led the men to the river and they speared the golden carp. Then they built great fires and cooked the fish. Everyone ate, hurrying to satisfy their hunger. And when they were done, they thanked Sipa for providing them with food.

Satisfied, they were ready to return to their homes when a storm descended on the valley. Lightning and a furious

wind lashed at the land; the people grew frightened. The dark clouds parted and they heard the voice of the Sun God. His voice sounded angry and loud as thunder.

"You have broken your promise!" the Sun God reminded them. "You have killed my fish, and now you must be punished! For what you have done, you will now become fish. You will never walk on the earth again."

"Forgive us," the people cried, falling to the ground. "It is Sipa who is to blame."

"Yes, I accept the blame," Sipa said. "I promised my father I would respect the golden fish of the river whose strength made my leg well. But you no longer answered my prayers. My people grew hungry. I had no choice."

"Each of you is responsible," the Sun God replied. "The people cannot put all the blame on the leader."

Sipa watched in terror as the Sun God changed his people into golden fish and tossed them into the river.

He stood on the bank alone, watching the fish-people swim in the muddy waters. The fish-people grew fearful in the cold river. Without a leader, they swam this way and that, losing all sense of direction.

"Help us," they cried to Sipa on the bank. "In this dark world of water, we will die! Help us!"

The Sun God turned to Sipa. "You forgot the vow you made to your father. Now you see the consequences."

"Forgive me," Sipa said. "You brought us to this place, and you healed my leg. I forgot my duty to you. Turn me into a fish also, so I may lead them to safe waters. Without me, they will perish in the dark currents."

The Sun God admired Sipa. Even though he had broken his promise, he was still willing to help his people.

"Very well," the Sun God said, "go and lead your people into the safety of the still ponds."

He turned Sipa into a huge, brilliant fish, whose presence lit the dark waters. He became the Golden Carp, king of the River of the Sun. He led his fish-people to a safe pond in the river, a new home.

Rain began to fall in the mountains, and the streams rushed into the River of the Sun. Soon the valley was green and lush again.

The fish-people followed their leader, the brilliant Golden Carp, up and down the river. Their bright orange color reflected the color of the sun, which daily shone down to illuminate their way.

Coyote and Raven

Long ago when the earth was young, First Man and First Woman lived in a dark cavern in the underworld. It was very damp and gloomy. First Man and First Woman were not only uncomfortable; they were frightened as well by the sounds of the ghosts and sorcerers who also lived in that dark world.

First Man and First Woman believed the earth was a turtle swimming around the sun. They had heard stories that on the turtle's shell existed a very different world. Badgers and moles who dug holes through the shell had brought word that the surface was bathed in light.

First Man and First Woman dreamed of breaking through the turtle shell. They yearned to live in a world of light, but they did not know how to pursue their dream.

One day when First Woman was out looking for tubers to eat, she found a hole that Badger had dug to the surface of the earth. It was a large hole, and First Woman thought Badger had hidden some food there.

"Maybe I can find Badger's potatoes and have them for my soup," she said.

Poking her head through the hole, First Woman saw a brilliant light that almost blinded her. For a moment, she was frightened, thinking one of the evil sorcerers had bewitched her and taken her sight away. She blinked and realized she was seeing the outside world. She saw a green forest, a river, and many animals.

"Ah, the badgers and the moles have told the truth," she said. "There is a bright world on the turtle's shell, and it's much nicer than our dark home in the cave."

Just then, Badger returned home. Seeing First Woman looking out through his hole, he quickly covered it, sprinkling dirt in her eyes.

First Woman threw a stick at Badger, then hurried off home to tell her husband what she had seen.

"First Man," she said, "I looked through Badger's hole to the surface of the earth. The world above is full of light, not dark and gloom like this one. It is covered with trees, a flowing river, and blue sky. Why don't we go live there?"

"It has always been our desire to live on the surface of the

earth, on the turtle shell," First Man said. "But how can we get there?"

"We can't use Badger's hole, for he has covered it up. Maybe we can climb up the side of the cave," she said.

"I tried it once," First Man said, "but it is too steep."

"Well, let us shout for help. Maybe one of the animals I saw on the upper world will help us."

First Man agreed. He knew his wife was usually right about such things.

In those times, all the animals were brothers and sisters. They shared the earth and lived in peace with one another. Each animal had its own nature and lived according to it.

Coyote and Raven were tricksters who were always getting in trouble. The pranks they pulled were the cause of Skunk smelling bad, of Rattlesnake losing his legs and having to slither along the ground, and of Deer stealing Rabbit's antlers.

The same day that First Man and First Woman decided to call for help, Coyote and Raven were walking near the cave that led to the underworld. As they paused to drink from a spring near the entrance, they were surprised to hear voices coming from the cave.

"Please help get us out of here," the voice pleaded.

"Who are you?" Coyote called back.

"Man and Woman," came the reply. "We want to come and live in your world. If you help us, we will reward you."

For Coyote and Raven, a reward usually meant a good feast, as they were always hungry.

"What will you give us?" Raven asked.

"I'll give you some tasty potato soup I just made," answered First Woman.

"I've never tasted potato soup," the starving Coyote said. "Let's go find Owl and see if he can help."

They ran to Owl, one of the wisest creatures in the forest.

"We heard the voices of Man and Woman, who live beneath the earth," Coyote told Owl. "They want to come and live with us on the shell of the turtle."

"And Woman promised us a bowl of soup," Raven added, holding his growling stomach. "We want to help them."

"You must be prepared for many changes if Man and Woman come to live here," said Owl.

"They will be like brother and sister to us," Coyote said, ignoring the warning. "Tell us what to do."

"Very well. Climb on my wings, and I'll take you there. But hold tight. There are many dangers when one travels to the underworld."

So Coyote climbed on one wing and Raven climbed on the other wing, and Owl flew down to the large cavern where they had heard the voices.

On the way down, the heart of the earth pounded so loudly, they had to fill their ears with wax.

They came to a river of fire erupting with molten lava.

Raven poked holes in the turtle's shell to let some of the lava escape so they could cross. Those holes in the earth are now called volcanoes.

Soon they came to that dark place where First Man and First Woman lived. They were pale as ghosts because they had never been in sunlight.

"Help us break through the turtle shell," First Man said.

Coyote said, "First feed us some of that delicious soup you promised us."

First Woman apologized. "I'm sorry, but you took so long in coming that we ate it all."

Raven and Coyote grew angry. They were about to return to the surface of the earth alone.

But First Man suggested another reward. "We can give you something of greater value than potato soup."

"What?" the sly Coyote asked.

"In the future, we will honor you by telling stories about you," First Man said. "Around our campfires we will tell our children how you helped us. Even the hundredth generation will know how you brought us to earth."

"What else?" Raven asked.

"You will be known as the best tricksters in the animal world. All your adventures will be told by our people."

Coyote and Raven liked the idea. Already they were known in the upper world for their pranks, but Man and Woman were promising them honor: Their exploits would live forever in the memory of the people.

"We want to help these two," they said to Owl.

"I can't carry them on my back," Owl said. "They are too heavy."

"What can we do?"

"Let us go back to the surface and make a plan," Owl said.

They returned to the surface, narrowly escaping the river of lava and the pounding of the earth's heart.

"I won't go that route again," Raven said. The exploding lava had nearly singed his feathers, which in those days were brightly colored.

"Nor I," Coyote agreed, taking the wax out of his ears. "I can barely hear. Let Man and Woman stay in the underworld."

"We gave our word to help them," Owl reminded them. "I have an idea."

"What?" the two tricksters asked.

Owl turned to Raven. "With your beak, peck at the turtle shell and make a large hole."

So Raven pecked and pecked, making a hole.

"Now, Coyote, stick your tail into the opening, and Man and Woman will grab it. When you feel their tug, pull very hard."

In those days, Coyote had a tail as long as a giraffe's neck. The shiny, fluffy fur was the envy of all the fur-bearing animals.

So Coyote stuck his shining tail down the hole, and soon he felt a tug. Man and Woman had grabbed his tail.

"The heart of the earth makes a pounding noise," Man and Woman cried in terror.

"Put wax in your ears!" Coyote shouted.

They did as they were told, and that is why even today men and women have wax in their ears.

Coyote pulled and pulled, and Man and Woman came through the opening to the surface of the earth.

Unfortunately, the evil sorcerers who lived in the dark underworld also grabbed Coyote's tail, and they, too, came to live on the earth. They dressed themselves in the skins of animals to escape detection.

On the surface, Man and Woman at first were blinded by the sunlight. Slowly, they got used to the bright light, and they looked around and admired the beauty of the earth.

"We thank you for helping us," they said to Coyote and Raven. "We will honor you by telling our children how you helped us come to this world."

That night, Man and Woman slept on earth for the first time. They covered themselves with leaves and were warm, but they couldn't sleep soundly. The following morning, they were in a bad mood.

"Why do we feel so grumpy?" First Woman asked.

"I had no dreams last night," replied First Man.

"That's it! We left our dreams in the underworld! Without our dreams, we will never be happy. We will have no visions of the future. Let's go to Coyote and Raven to see if they can help."

They went to the two tricksters and explained the problem.

"We love this earth," First Woman said, "but in our hurry to grab your tail, we left our dreams in the underworld. Can you retrieve them for us?"

Coyote and Raven were busy eating a watermelon.

"It is too dangerous to go back only for dreams," Coyote said. "Learn to live without dreaming."

And so Man and Woman went off to create many tribes on the face of the earth. All gave thanks to the sun for bringing them sight and life, and all told the story of how Coyote and Raven helped First Man and First Woman come to the world.

As the tribes increased, they learned to live in harmony with nature, but still they felt something missing. First Man and First Woman had passed on their stories but not their dreams. Without these dreams, there were no visions of the future.

Coyote and Raven continued to help Man and Woman. They taught them to hunt and fish and gather grains and nuts. They taught them to respect their home, the earth. They taught them that from the smallest to the greatest, every living thing was part of creation.

Even when the two tricksters got into trouble, there was a lesson to be learned from their antics. First Man and First Woman often laughed and told stories about Coyote and Raven, realizing that in each story there was a valuable lesson.

The evil sorcerers who had sneaked up from the underworld grew jealous. By having stories told about their exploits, Coyote and Raven had become powerful. As long as Coyote and Raven existed, the sorcerers couldn't control the many tribes.

"Let us plot the downfall of Raven and Coyote," the leader of the sorcerers said. "Then we will have our way with the people."

"Coyote and Raven get into a lot of trouble," another sorcerer answered, "but the people admire them because of the lessons they teach. They are too powerful."

"We must have that power," the leader said. "And so we must creep into the hearts of the people and turn them against one another."

The sorcerers set out to spread envy and jealousy, and soon the tribes no longer trusted one another. Arguments and squabbles erupted everywhere.

"The tribes are fighting with one another," Coyote said to Raven.

"Let them," he answered. "When they go off to make war, they leave their food unguarded. Then I eat like a king."

"Yes, but when they are fighting, they no longer tell stories of our exploits. If the people no longer tell stories about us, we lose our power."

"You're right," Raven said. "They promised to remember us in the stories. Now they no longer have time. We must stop the fighting and squabbling—for our own good."

So Coyote and Raven called for a gathering of the tribes at the foot of Taos Mountain. The tribes came from all over to attend the powwow. From the eastern plains they came; from the west near the ocean they came. From as far north as Alaska they came, and from Mexico to the south they came.

When they were gathered, Coyote and Raven spoke. "You must stop your fighting and arguing. You must live in peace and harmony. Always remember to tell your stories to your children. If there is no storytelling, then your children will not learn the ways of your ancestors. Soon they will have no memory of the past, and they will lose their way."

"Coyote and Raven are right," the elders said. "We must never stop telling the children our stories. This is the only way they have to learn our history, traditions, and religion."

The people agreed to put aside their differences, and for a while there was peace.

The sorcerers grew angry. "That meddlesome Coyote and Raven have thwarted our plan. The people are living in peace, and they entertain and teach their children by telling them stories. Coyote and Raven have power again, and the people hate us because of our evil ways."

"We must turn Coyote and Raven against each other," their leader said. "If the people see them fighting, they, too, will fall back to arguing and bickering. People who don't love their neighbors are easy prey. Soon we will control their hearts."

So the sorcerers devised a contest. They sent many fleet-footed deer to call Coyote and Raven and the tribes to another gathering near Taos Mountain. When all were assembled, the leader of the sorcerers spoke.

"We must have a contest to decide who is the best trickster, Coyote or Raven."

The people loved contests, so all waited eagerly. Nobody recognized the sorcerers dressed in the skins of animals.

"Tell me what I have to do and I'll do it," Coyote said. He considered himself to be king of the tricksters.

"You are to return to the center of the earth to retrieve the dreams of First Man and First Woman. You know that in their haste to climb your tail, they left their dreams behind."

"This is a good idea," said First Man. "We would honor the trickster who brings our dreams back."

Owl hooted a warning. "Be careful, Coyote and Raven. This is a trick to turn you against each other."

Coyote and Raven didn't pay attention to Owl. Each wanted to be king of the tricksters.

"I'm a better trickster than Coyote," Raven bragged. "Let me go first."

Without waiting, he flew down the hole he had pecked long ago. He heard the pounding of the earth's heart, and he flew over the molten lava. When he came to the former home of First Man and First Woman, he saw their dreams lying very orderly on the ground.

He gathered up all the dreams he could carry in his beak and started back, but as he crossed the river of lava, there was a loud explosion. Burning boulders and streams of fire filled the cavern.

Raven squawked in fear as the hot lava singed his feathers. The dreams fell from his beak, and he quickly gathered some up. He picked them up in such a hurry, the dreams became all jumbled. That's why dreams today often appear as mixed-up images.

He flew to the surface as fast as he could, leaving many dreams behind.

"Here are your dreams," Raven said when he arrived on the surface, giving those dreams he had brought to First Man.

"But these are all mixed up," First Man said. "They don't make sense. How are we to know what is truly in our hearts?"

"He made a mess, all right," Coyote said. "And look at him. His feathers got burned!"

It was true: Raven's once-bright rainbow feathers were black as coal.

"I warned you," Owl said, but everyone was so busy laughing at Raven, no one heard him.

"I am the better trickster," Coyote said. "I will bring back the dreams that Raven left behind."

He wrapped his beautiful long tail around a tree and climbed down the hole. He picked up the remaining dreams and carefully made his way around the hot lava. When the sorcerers saw he was about to succeed, they cut his tail, and Coyote fell back down the hole. Bruised and battered, he quickly gathered as many dreams as he could, but they, too, were jumbled.

He scrambled to the surface and gave the dreams to the people. Some laughed when they saw Coyote's short, scraggy tail.

"You have made a mess of things," First Man said. "We were supposed to give a dream to each tribe, so they might have true visions. But now the dreams are confusing."

Nevertheless, Man and Woman, who were grandfather and grandmother by now, gave a dream to each tribe.

"Each of you must find your dream and follow it," they told the tribes. "Your dream will be a vision to guide your life."

The tribes were thankful, but they soon learned that to have true vision didn't come easily. It took a great deal of understanding and knowledge.

The people chased Coyote and Raven away. Never again would the two live in human houses.

Unfortunately, Coyote and Raven didn't learn their lesson. Each one still thinks he is the king of the tricksters. To this day, they go on arguing and pulling tricks on each other. And the sorcerers remain on earth, constantly plotting how to turn people against one another.

First Man and First Woman did keep their promise. Even today, when families gather in a warm kitchen in the winter, many stories are told about Coyote and Raven.

The tribes retain the stories of their ancestors. As long as the stories are told, the people know their history, and dreams and visions help guide each person on the good path their ancestors taught.

Glossary

abuelo • *grandfather*

adiós • *good-bye*

adobe • *sun-dried mud bricks*

Agua Negra • *the name of a place, but literally means "black water"*

amigo • *friend*

bolas de lumbre • *balls of fire*

bosque • *forest*

buenas noches • *good night*

buenas tardes • *good afternoon*

bueno • *good*

buenos días • *good day*

compadre • *godfather—one who has baptized or confirmed a child or who has been a best man at a wedding; also, friend*

conquistador • *conqueror*

corrido • *ballad*

cuento • *folktale, also story*

curandero • *healer*

Dios mío • *oh, my God*

este perro loco • *this crazy dog*

fiesta • *party*

gracias • *thank you*

gracias a Dios • *thanks be to God*

Kookoóee • *bogeyman (Kookoóee is the phonetic spelling of Cucúi, which means Coco.)*

la muerte • *death*

Llano Estacado • *plains of eastern New Mexico*

luna • *moon*
mercado • *marketplace*
mi hija, hijo • *my daughter, son*
muchacho malo • *bad boy*
muy bien • *very good*
muy bravo • *very angry, wild,*
 or brave
pícaro • *rascal*
pobre gallina • *poor chicken*
pueblo • *village*

ranchito • *small ranch*
rico • *rich man*
sala • *living room*
seguro que sí • *of course*
señora, señor • *Mrs., Mr.*
vamos • *let's go*
vaquero • *cowboy*
vecino • *neighbor*
viejo • *old man*